Kathleen,
May the
Bless you
measure!

Richard

A Touch of Grace

Richard G. Arno, Ph.D.

*"A Book of
Encouragement"*

35th Anniversary
NCCA
Louisville, Ky.
Marriott

2016
10/28

Finally, brethren,
whatsoever things are true,
whatsoever things are honest,
whatsoever things are just,
whatsoever things are pure,
whatsoever things are lovely,
whatsoever things are of good report;
if there be any virtue,
and if there be any praise,
think on these things.

Philippians 4:8 (KJV)

SCRIPTURE REFERENCES

Except where noted all scripture references
in this book are taken from the
King James Version of the Holy Bible.

TABLE OF CONTENTS

Introduction
Dedication
Title Selection

INTRODUCTION
By
Donald L. Struble, D.B.A.

If I have ever seen the faith of parents imparted to a son or daughter, I've seen it in the Arno family. The faith in the Lordship of Jesus Christ, found active in the lives of Mom and Dad Arno, Marion and Clarence, was a demonstrated role model for their son Richard. This book communicates the power of faith demonstrated and faith believed.

I've had the honor of knowing Marion and Clarence Arno, and observing their great love for the Lord in their daily practice. Now, they have both personally beheld the Glory of His heavenly presence, fulfilling once again the personal prayer of Jesus which is found in John, Chapter 17, verse 24, saying: "whom Thou hast given Me, be with Me where I am, in order that they may behold My glory."

Likewise, I've been blessed to be a close friend of the author, Dr. Richard Arno. I have been close enough to observe his own powerful faith, some of which is revealed to you through this book. Dr. Arno's testimony and truths, which leap off these pages, will increase your own enthusiasm for Christ and His Spirit. It is a personal relationship with his Rescuer that spurs him on to higher levels of accomplishment day-by-day, year-by-year.

If you are a person who considers your own life and future by daily exercise and taking daily vitamins, let me challenge you to do the following: Read a title a day and meditate on that subject. There are enough titles to take you through a month or two! Then, begin the discipline over again.

This is a great spiritual exercise program. As you read each of the subjects taken from Dr. Arno's personal life experiences, let these words build you up and strengthen you in your Christian faith. Truly, this book is not a "once through and shelve it" story book, but rather a spiritual "vitamin" and exercise handbook which will increase your own level of faith, as the real life drama has done for Dr. Arno.

Become a man or woman of great faith yourself. It's a decision.

This book would be a great gift for ministers and public speakers who appreciate having "sermon/message starters" and enjoy sharing stories, anecdotes, and metaphors.

DEDICATION

I dedicate this book to the Lord Jesus Christ, my Savior and Redeemer-my Healer and Majestic Lord.

I also dedicate this book to my wife, Phyllis, who is a God-send. She is a wonderful partner, co-worker, lover and best friend. Without her support, encouragement and hard work, this book would have been impossible to write.

My three children, Rick, Jaysen and Erin have brought honor to me because of who they have become, through Jesus Christ. To them, I impart the blessings of the Lord, which He has showered upon me throughout my life.

Finally, I want to give a special acknowledgment to my mother and father, Clarence and Marion Arno. They taught me that I have a friend in Jesus. The person I have become is because of Him and because of their love, encouragement and support. I honestly do not know who I would be today if they had not taught me the Holy Scriptures and encouraged me to live a life that would bring glory to His name.

TITLE SELECTION

When my father surrendered to the Lord's command and obediently reached to "touch" me, God's grace filled my hospital room.

My parents said that: "The presence of God's grace was so beautiful that it could only be described as Shekinah Glory."

Indeed, my healing and my entire life has been "A Touch of Grace." I selected this as my title in order to boldly declare what God has done for me.

PART ONE

HIS GRACE ABOUNDS

Scripture Reference: Isa. 53:4-5

My birthday was on December 21st. It was 1972 and the church I was pastoring had many activities scheduled. We had a church bus and the young people, under my leadership, were going Christmas caroling every night until Christmas.

I had only been the pastor for six months. It was quite an opportunity, the kind ministers would consider a promotion. This was a station church meaning that the church fully supported at least one full-time pastor. I went there from West Virginia where I pastored two churches, which the United Methodist Church calls a charge or a circuit.

I felt myself becoming more and more committed to the "cause" of Christ and less committed to the person of Jesus Christ. Good works tend to become an end in themselves. I was very busy doing all the right things, but seemed to be lacking a sense of spiritual peace.

That evening, December 21, 1972, I remained at the church by myself. The teens had left, and our evening of celebrating

Jesus' birth by caroling throughout the community had come to an end.

I stayed at the church because, for the third day in a row, I had a severe headache and needed to be alone with the Lord to pray. As I stood in the sanctuary with all of the lights off except for the one over the pulpit, I asked Him to heal me. However, in the same prayer, I admitted to Him that I was not sure if I even believed in divine healing.

After I left the church that night my headaches became even more severe. The pain was unlike any I had ever had experienced. I would pin myself between both ends of the sofa and press on the top of my head in order to relieve some of the pressure. However, nothing I did reduced the pain. I was taking over-the-counter pain pills with no effect. Up to this point I was perfectly healthy. At age thirty, the only medical problem I had ever experienced was a mild case of Chicken Pox.

On the day after Christmas, I slipped into a coma. My family took me from one hospital to another in an attempt to find out what was wrong. Many doctors insinuated that I was probably taking drugs. Others suspected that I was in a drunken stupor. However, one neurologist who examined me knew right away that I was in a coma and that I had a severe brain disease. From there I was taken to Duke University Medical Center in Durham, North Carolina.

Spinal taps and E.E.G.'s revealed that I had spinal meningitis and viral encephalitis. My family was called in and I was placed on what was referred to as the "death floor." At that time it was 3-West. This is where they place a terminal person and keep them as comfortable as possible until they expire.

My family was allowed to view me through a port-hole, but I was in total isolation, and no one, other than hospital staff, was allowed in my room. My temperature rose to 108° and remained there for three days. My brain hemorrhaged in three major areas; on the top, on the right side at my temple, and in the back near the base of my skull. The brain damage was severe and my condition was terminal. My family was given no hope.

My mother and father were Christians and they placed all of their trust in Jesus. They believed in divine healing and in the power of prayer.

Over 150 of my church members packed in cars and busses and made their way to Duke Medical Center to lend their support to my devastated family. I was the youngest of three children. My family had never experienced anything to compare to this tragedy and certainly needed the support of other Christians.

When the church members arrived they met my family in the Duke Medical Center lobby. Since my mother and father had such a deep faith in God's love and in His healing power, the first thing they did was bring everyone together into a huge prayer circle. They occupied nearly the entire lobby, and it was quite a testimony to everyone's faith.

While they were praying, my primary care physician tapped my father on the back and called him out of the prayer circle. He said: "You people are making fools of yourselves! If you believe that there is a God and that He is a God of mercy, you should be asking Him to let that boy die." He went on to explain that there were only thirty known cases of my type of viral encephalitis–that it was very rare.

Of the thirty known cases, twenty-six patients never regained consciousness. They died while in a coma. The other four were left with massive brain damage and required constant care. I was case number thirty-one and already considered little more than a vegetable.

My father just looked at the doctor and said: "Our God heals." At that point he turned his back on the doctor and re-joined the prayer circle.

The next day my mother and father went to this doctor and told him that they wanted to enter my room. He was adamantly against this and denied their request. My father, a road contractor, however, was quite insistent and the doctor finally agreed. He approved the visit on two conditions. First, they had to agree to wear all of the isolation equipment that he required and second, that they would not touch me. They agreed to both conditions.

I was strapped down with six-inch leather straps over both wrists, over my abdomen and over both ankles. As they stood in my room looking at me they remembered how healthy I had been only a week before and were filled with helplessness and despair. Then, the Lord spoke very clearly to my father and instructed him to "touch me." He resisted because he had given the doctor his word that he would not touch me. However, the Lord was insistent and promised my father that if he would touch me, He would heal me.

Not really knowing whether he was doing right or wrong, he, with child-like faith, began stretching out his hands toward my chest. Before he actually touched me, the room filled with what my father and mother called God's Shekinah glory. The Lord never made my father break the promise. He only required him to declare "in whom he placed his trust."

With the room filled with the presence of God, my mother and father quietly backed out of the room in awe. They announced to everyone that the Lord was present in my room and that He was there to take me home or to heal me. They surrendered to His will and a peace began to permeate all of them.

About six hours later I AWOKE!

There was a doctor in my room and I began asking him questions–questions that he first thought were mere murmurings of a hallucinating patient. My questions, however, were direct and intelligent and he finally realized that I had emerged from the coma. Within ten minutes he had about eighteen doctors in my room examining me. They could not find any sign of brain damage. My temperature was back to normal, my blood pressure was perfect and all my vital signs were stable. They were astounded and left the room to collect their data.

After they left, I can remember looking out the window of my third floor hospital room and seeing a man delivering soft drinks to the hospital. He backed the truck up, slid open one of the side doors and started stacking crates of soft drinks onto a hand truck. As I stood watching him, I experienced a love I had never known. He was a living soul and for a moment, God allowed me to feel the love He had for that soul. It was an overwhelming feeling which I could hardly contain. I knew wholeheartedly that God loved that man and wanted to be loved by him. This was my first experience after coming out of the coma.

The day after I awoke from the coma, a seminar was scheduled at the Duke Medical Center. Over 125 neurologists were to meet and discuss specific cases. My doctor asked if it would be all right to use me and my records as one of their primary case studies. I was delighted with the request and granted my consent.

During the seminar, they copied and provided each neurologist with my medical report up to the time I emerged from the coma. They were given about one hour to review the case and determine my present state. They all agreed that I was either dead or still in the coma. At that point, I walked in the room. They all stood and applauded.

They asked me questions for what seemed to be two or three hours and then I left. At that point, they were given the balance of my medical records and asked to continue their review. Their assignment was to form a medical conclusion to explain my recovery.

Towards the end of the day, three medical doctors came to my room to share the results of the review. They said that all the neurologists agreed that I should be told, in laymen's terms, exactly what happened to me. They said that it was as though I had cut off my right arm, taken two aspirins, lain down for an hour and grown a new arm. They also told me that everyone present believed that I was "healed by an act of divine power."

I was 100% healed except for one problem. My vision was blurry. They took me to the Duke University Eye Clinic and examined me. After the examination, they explained that the optic nerve in both eyes had been destroyed, probably due to my high temperature. It was inoperable, and they told me that, I was legally blind. I would be unable to drive an automobile or cross a street without assistance.

That night, I vividly remember kneeling by my hospital bed. I also remember the prayer I prayed:

> *"Father, I want to reach as many people for Jesus during my life as I can. If I can reach one thousand lost souls as a blind man and only 999 with my vision, Father, I beg you, for that one soul, let me stay blind. If I can reach one thousand lost souls with my vision restored and only 999 as a blind man, Father, I beg you, for that one soul, restore my vision."*

When I climbed into bed, I experienced the greatest peace I have ever known. Indeed, it was a peace "that passeth all understanding" and a joy "unspeakable." I knew that God was going to use me at my maximum potential and that He would decide which way He could use me best.

The next morning I opened the door to my hospital room and looked down the long hall. There, hundreds of feet away, I saw a sign that read EXIT. It was crystal clear and brilliant. My vision was totally restored. The reading glasses I once needed were like binoculars and had to be discarded.

Now, at every opportunity, I boldly proclaim my belief in divine healing! My God heals! God heals!

PART TWO

METAPHORS, SIMILES, STORIES & ALLEGORIES

The following are some metaphors, similes, stories and allegories that I have read or heard throughout my forty-plus years of full-time Christian service. They have impacted my life and the ministry God has entrusted to my care.

I may have read some of them in Christian magazines, some in my college textbooks, or perhaps I heard them from a pulpit somewhere. I cannot be sure of their source so I can only list them as "author unknown" and "source unknown."

These are precious stories and I pray that God truly blesses the authors and those who are responsible for passing them on to me (through the years) so that I can, in the Spirit of Jesus Christ, pass them on to you.

It's too heavy daddy!

Subjects: Knowledge/Limitations/Responsibility/
Trust
Scripture Reference: Ps. 139:6

A businessman was on a commuter train heading towards New York with his six-year-old daughter accompanying him. With his briefcase open, he shuffled through his important papers while his little girl thumbed through magazines that were strewn about the railway car.

As they neared the end of their journey, the little girl asked: "Daddy, what is sex?" She probably saw the word in one of the magazines she was browsing and her question startled her father. How could he respond to such a question from a six year old in such a way as to bring forth good rather than evil?

The announcement came over the loudspeaker just then declaring, "Main Street, New York," which was where they were to disembark. The train began to slow down. Her father pushed his heavy suitcase toward the little girl and said: "Honey, will you carry this for daddy?" She responded: "Oh, yes, daddy!" As she reached down and grabbed the handle, she tugged and pulled and tugged and pulled; and, with a sigh, she said: "Daddy, I can't! It is just too heavy!"

Her dad looked at her and said: "Honey, that suitcase is just like the answer to your question. It is too heavy for you to carry right now; but when you get older and stronger, you will be able to carry knowledge that you're too little to carry right now.

When you are old enough and strong enough, I will entrust the answer to you. Until then, I will carry it for you."

As human beings we have limited comprehension. We may ask "Why did God take my loved one away from me? Why did I lose my health? Why did I lose my job?" The Lord does not answer many of our questions because we, as humans, are not capable of carrying that knowledge; it is just too heavy.

The Bible tells us: "Lean not unto thine own understanding." Proverbs 3:5. Yet, that is the very thing we attempt to do when we ask, even demand, answers from God.

A misperception

**Subjects: Misperception/Misunderstanding/
Relationships (Broken)/Truth**
Scripture Reference: Jn. 8:32

A young man, in his early twenties, and his father went to a counselor in need of help. They just could not get along–it was as though the young man detested his father and could hardly stand the sight of him. There was no apparent reason for such an attitude. The father tried to be a good and loving father. He took great interest in the young man's life as he was growing up and was an excellent provider.

After many sessions, which all seemed to be in vain, a breakthrough came. Although the memory was suppressed, through therapy it was brought to the surface. The son told the therapist about an incident that took place when he was about six years old. His appendix ruptured and he was taken to the emergency room by ambulance. His father was notified and he rushed to the hospital as quickly as possible. When he arrived, the young man was already being prepared for emergency surgery. Just at the precise moment when ether was being administered, the father literally busted into the operating room. He was shouting "I don't want him!"

That was the very last words the boy heard before the anesthesia took effect and it was devastating for him to learn that his father did not want him. Hearing this was so painful that the young man buried the actual memory. However, his overt behavior clearly indicated that he knew the truth about how his father despised him.

The therapist asked the father why he despised the boy so much that he would boldly and publicly proclaim that he did not want him. The father, with tears in his eyes, responded: "I was talking about the doctor! He was an alcoholic and I was not about to let him touch my son, whom I loved and needed so very, very much."

The garment of Jesus The Lamb!

**Subjects: Eternal Life/Grace/Hope/Mercy/
            Salvation**
Scripture Reference: Jn. 14: 6

A pastor and evangelist named Rev. Harry Ironside, who was from the Chicago area, was invited to conduct a revival for a church in Texas.

During the week-long revival, he was invited to share meals with different members of the congregation. One evening after his meal at the home of a Texas rancher something happened that had a tremendous influence on his life and ministry.

The rancher invited him to go for a walk on the range. They had plenty of time before the evening service, so Rev. Ironside was delighted to accept the offer. As they walked and talked about some of their experiences and enjoyed each other's company, they passed a flock of sheep.

Rev. Ironside could not help but notice that one of the little lambs had two front feet, two hind feet and two heads. He asked the rancher if lambs were often born with such hideous birth defects. The rancher's reply was shocking. He stated: "Rev. Ironside, that little lamb was not born that way. In fact, that is one of the most beautiful things that has ever happened on this ranch!"

He went on to explain that one morning, when he and the other hired hands went out to check on the sheep, they found a dead ewe. Apparently, she was in the process of giving birth during the night when she started hemorrhaging and died. The lamb survived and was cuddled up next to the dead ewe. That same morning, they found another ewe that gave birth to a stillborn lamb. This left them with a ewe that had no lamb and a lamb that had no mother.

They corralled the ewe and placed the baby lamb inside the coral with her in the hopes that she would nurse the lamb that had no mother. However, when she looked at the lamb, even though it was beautiful, she knew that it was not hers and she started charging it. They rescued the lamb just in time. One of the hired hands went back out on the range to find the carcass of the lamb that died during birth. He removed the organs and took the outer carcass back to the coral. Then he tied the carcass on to the little lamb that had no mother. Indeed, it was the ugliest thing one could imagine. Nevertheless, when the ewe saw the little lamb, she recognized that it was hers and immediately went to it and allowed it to nurse.

Rev. Ironside listened to the rancher as he shared this miraculous event and he came to understand that it provides a perfect spiritual parallel. No matter how beautiful or good a person is, if placed in the presence of our infinite God, He will simply say, "depart from me, I do not know you." His acceptance has absolutely nothing to do with goodness, outer or inner beauty. However, if you take another person, even one who is filthy, and wrap the garment of Jesus Christ around him, when they enter into the presence of God, He says, "Behold, my son."

Our only hope is Jesus. Goodness will not help us and righteousness will not help us. When we go into the presence of God, if He does not see us clothed in the garment of Jesus we will be told to depart!

Long handled spoon

**Subjects: Giving/Heaven/Hell/Selfishness/
             Sharing**
Scripture Reference: Lk. 6: 38

A man died and went to Heaven. When he arrived, several people greeted him and asked him if he would like to go with them on a tour of the universe. "Of course," he replied, and everyone began loading up on busses.

The first place they went was to Hell. The man described it saying that Hell was a giant banquet hall, and down the center of the hall was a giant banqueting table. It was covered with food–everything that you could imagine. It was a feast!

The Heavenly tourist said that he could not understand what he was seeing and hearing. Right in the midst of this magnificent banquet, everyone seemed to be starving. Everyone was very angry and extremely frustrated. They had food in their hair, all over their faces and they were cursing and screaming. He looked more closely to see why they were not eating and why they were so unhappy.

He noticed that all of them had their left arm tied behind their back and a six-foot spoon strapped to their right arm. What a predicament! All that food, and to be so hungry and not be able to get any of it in your mouth!

At this point, the Heavenly tourist climbed back onto the bus with the others. Their next stop was Heaven. When the man entered into Heaven, he found an exact duplicate of the large banquet hall and banqueting table that he witnessed in Hell. This time, however, everyone was laughing and having a wonderful time! Upon examination he realized that all of these people also had their left hands tied behind their backs and a six-foot spoon strapped to their right arms.

The difference? The people in Heaven had learned how to feed one another! This, my friend, is the secret to happiness and a fulfilled life. It is also the secret to happy and lifelong relationships. When we care more about others than we do ourselves, we will attain happiness, true happiness–abundantly!

Denying Christ

Subjects: Confessing Christ/Denial/Eternal Life/ Mercy/ Salvation/Testifying
Scripture Reference: Mt. 10: 32-33

Peter Cartwright was a circuit rider. He was one of the great men who helped to establish Christianity in America when in its infancy. Most towns were small and could not support a full-time preacher so the preacher would go from town to town staying about a week in each location while he ministered to the needs of that community. A circuit rider like Peter Cartwright would travel from town to town on horseback. One day, when he was scheduled to leave for the next town, he was delayed as he attempted to help someone in need. He was not sure if he could make it before sunset and he knew he could not ride at night; nevertheless, he felt it was worth a try.

After completing about three-fourths of the journey, it became too dangerous to continue, so he stopped for the night. He rested beside a large tree and used a stone for his pillow. That night Peter Cartwright had a dream which he recorded in his personal diary.

In his dream, he died. He found himself laying face down in front of the throne of God. He heard a voice from the throne say "arise and state your name." He attempted to stand but was unable to do so. The voice came a second time but still, he was unable to move or respond. Finally, he heard the voice say "arise and state your name or be cast into outer darkness."

Peter Cartwright knew that this would be his last opportunity and he tried with all of his might to move. However, with every ounce of energy he had, he was unable to move a muscle. He just lay there in total hopelessness, knowing that he could not act in his own defense. At what seemed to be his last moment, he looked out from the corner of his eyes and he saw what he described as "two sandaled feet." He felt two strong hands on his arm raising him to a standing position. Then, he heard the most beautiful words he ever heard in his life.

The man with the sandaled feet said: "Father, I want to introduce you to Peter Cartwright, a man who knew me and boldly declared me as Lord. He faithfully served me all the days of his life."

In that moment, Peter Cartwright knew full well the meaning of Matthew 10:32-33: "Whosoever therefore shall confess me before men, him will I confess also before my father which is in Heaven. But whosoever shall deny me before men, him will I also deny before my father which is in Heaven." Declare Him at every opportunity and make opportunities to declare Him.

This was the very last story my mother heard me tell. One evening she attended a conference where I was speaking and the next day she, quite unexpectedly, suffered a heart attack and died. I am sure she heard the same words that Rev. Cartwright heard from the lips of the Lord–the one with the sandaled feet.

Procrusteanism

Subjects: Control/Manipulation/Molds/ Obsessiveness
Scripture Reference: Gen. 1: 26

There is a term from Greek mythology called PROCRUS-TEANISM. A story was told in ancient Greece about a man named Procrustees. This man would invite friends and neighbors to his home for the weekend as his special guest. These guests were only required to do one thing, to sleep in the Procrustean room. This room was equipped with a bed which all guests were required to fit "perfectly."

If you did not fit the bed because you were longer than the bed, then Procrustees would begin cutting you off from the legs up until you and the bed were the same length. If you were too short, then you were stretched to the correct length. The word procrusteanism was translated into English to mean "the obsession of making others fit your mold." The problem, you see, is that most of us suffer from procrusteanism.

We are diligent in our efforts to make others fit our mold. Likewise, we are diligent in our efforts to fit the mold that others have made for us. Children are trying to be exactly who their mother, father, friends and/or society molded them to be instead of being the person God created them to be. This is like an apple tree trying to grow oranges!

Refusing to compromise

**Subjects: Boldness/Compromise/Confidence/
Fearlessness/Responsibility/
Righteousness/Truth
Scripture Reference: Ps. 118: 6**

After Martin Luther posted his ninety-five theses on the front door of the church he was pastoring in Germany, he was called to Rome to appear before a high ranking Roman Catholic Church officer. In fact, some say that it was the Pope himself.

The church official said "Martin, I implore you to cease your activities in Germany." Luther was rocking the Roman Catholic Church's "boat" and they did not like it. He was a major threat to Catholicism.

Martin Luther's famous response has served to encourage me during some of my greatest temptations. Like all Christians, I have had many opportunities to "hide my light under a bushel" and to play in the political sandbox. Luther's response rings through the ages and serves as a reminder to us all. Will we serve God or man? He boldly responded: "Here I stand and God help me, I can do no other."

The atheist

Subjects: **Angels (Ministering) /Atheism/Denial/**
Divine Protection/Mercy/Prayer
Scripture Reference: Ps. 91: 10-11

Several men were sitting around a table in a pub talking when the subject of God came up. One of the men, a husky lumberjack, leaned back in his chair and said "That God stuff is a bunch of bunk. I don't believe there is a God."

One of the other men asked him why and he recounted the following event: "One day, I was lost in the wilderness in a blinding snow storm. I was hundreds of miles from the nearest settlement. I knew my only hope was to ask God for help, so I did. I prayed to God and asked Him to help me, but He did nothing! He can't exist. If there was a God, He would never have left me out there like that and ignored my prayers."

Everyone at the table sat in utter silence. After a moment or two of silence, the lumberjack asked what was wrong. One of the men said "Well, you are alive! How did you get out?" To that he replied, "Well God sure didn't help! An Eskimo appeared out of nowhere and took me to safety."

When we pray and ask God for help, sometimes He sends a stranger who "appears out of nowhere." Could the stranger be an Angel?

Penetrating theology

Subjects: Bible/Faith (Childlike)/Jesus/Love/Theology
Scripture Reference: Jn. 3: 16 & Jn. 15: 13

On one occasion, a reporter approached one of the world's greatest theologians, Carl Barth. He asked Barth to give him a theological statement which would encompass Barth's faith in Christ.

Of course, the reporter was expecting a complex dissertation–a deep theological, mind boggling response. Barth pondered for a second and then said:

> *"A theological statement that encompasses my faith?*
> *Jesus loves me, this I know, for the Bible tells me so."*

This, dear friend, is the most profound theological statement in Christianity. He first loved us! When theology and doctrine become more important to you than this central fact, you need to come home. Come home now.

The Island Theory

Subjects: Faith (Childlike)/Foolishness/Humility/
**   Knowledge/Reality**
Scripture Reference: I Cor. 13: 12 & Mk. 10: 15

Have you ever heard of the Circle of Knowledge? It is also referred to as the "Island Theory." Although Thomas Jefferson did not originate the theory, he stated it this way: "The more one knows, the more he realizes how little he knows."

You and I consider Albert Einstein a genius, but he considered himself an ignorant man. This can be explained in the Island Theory. If you could draw a circle which would encompass everything that you knew when you were eighteen years old, your circle would probably be quite small. Then, after you attend college, you could draw another circle. This circle would obviously have to be much larger because at this point, you know more than you did when you were eighteen. If you wait even longer, perhaps after marriage and rearing your children, you could draw a third circle and this one would be even larger than the second.

Do you see what is transpiring? As the circle gets larger and larger, expanding to encompass all that you know, so does the perimeter of the circle. The perimeter is adding new avenues that you previously did not even realize existed back when you graduated from high school.

As new avenues open up to you, you begin to realize that there are avenues that you have not even begun to travel and you realize how little you know. It is like living on a street in downtown Manhattan. If you have never been off that street, you know that street quite well. However, when you venture up to the corner and look to the North, East, South and West, it is quite humbling because you realize how much more exists beyond your tiny little street.

Albert Einstein was aware of avenues of thought, knowledge and information that you and I do not even know exists and this made him quite humble and left him feeling quite ignorant.

This entire theory can be applied to our relationship with God. The center of our faith is "Jesus loves me, this I know, for the

Bible tells me so." However, as we study and experience God as He interacts with man, questions begin to arise that challenge our childlike faith.

All our questions seem to lead us to answers which only birth more questions.

It is good to study, learn and develop in areas such as theology and doctrine, however, we must maintain our childlike faith. When we lose our childlike faith, we lose everything! Knowledge may work against us, and in the end, it will cause our damnation. We must remember that God chooses the foolish things to confound the wise. Our intellect, second only to Satan, may be our soul's worst enemy.

Just a pebble

Subjects: **Authority/ Destiny/Effecting Change/ Eternal Life/Evangelism/Obstacles/ Responsibility**

Scripture Reference: Mt. 17: 20b

There is a place up high in the Rocky Mountains called the Continental Divide. It is a spot where a small stream of water spews up out of the ground. As the water makes its way into the air it, by natural forces, falls back to the earth on the west side of the mountain. There, it joins a stream that ultimately makes its way into the Pacific ocean.

If a person strategically places a pebble about the size of a thumb nail on the hole in the rock where the water comes out, the water is deflected. Then, as it makes its way into the air, it falls back to earth, not on the west side of the mountain but on the east side. It then joins a different stream and ultimately makes its way to the Atlantic ocean.

How amazing that one small pebble, placed in the right place can change the destiny of the water. It is the same way with you. You say "What can I do, I am only one person?" If you are so much as a pebble in the hands of God, you can change the destiny of one or of thousands.

$\mathcal{A}$ resurrection sermon

**Subjects: Death/Hope/Jesus/Resurrection/Sin/Victory
Scripture Reference: Mt. 28: 1-7**

I attended a little country church one Sunday that was predominately African-American. I must say that I was never so privileged to hear such beautiful singing or such excellent preaching.

As the preacher addressed the congregation, his enthusiasm increased with every word. His conclusion regarding the resurrection of Jesus Christ went something like this: "Sin handed Jesus over to death and said 'okay death, I got him for you, now you hold him.' Then sin checked back on Saturday afternoon and asked death if he still had him. Death said 'you bet I have him–he ain't goin no where.' On Sunday morning, sin stopped by again and said 'Death, where's Jesus?'" With that, the old preacher jumped up, slammed his Bible down on the pulpit and shouted:

"That ole Death said to sin, I had him! I had him! But he got away!"

Feelings

**Subjects: Calvary/Confidence (In God)/Eternal Life/
Fact/Faith/Feeling/Trust
Scripture Reference: Isa. 12: 2**

FACT, FAITH and FEELING were walking on a wall. And FEELING took an awful fall. It pulled FAITH down, but FACT remained and pulled FAITH up and up came FEELING too! I FEEL just as good when I don't FEEL good as I do when I do FEEL good because I don't go by FEELINGS, I go by FACTS, and the FACTS don't change. The FACT is that Jesus died on Calvary so that we can have eternal life through Him. This FACT remains no matter how we FEEL. And the FACT is: Jehovah is our salvation! Trust Him!

No glory here!

**Subjects: Boldness/Humanism/Satan/
Self-exultation/Victory
Scripture Reference: Lk. 14: 11**

True Satan worshippers do not actually worship Satan. Like him, they, worship themselves. This is why humanism is a satanic religion. Self is at the center or focal point of humanism. Humanism (self-exaltation) is Satan's greatest weapon against humanity and Christ's Church.

In Luke 14:11 Jesus said: "For whosoever exalteth himself shall be abased; and he that humbleth himself shall be exalted." This scripture leaves little doubt as to what will happen to those who practice humanism (self-worship).

Humiliating Satan

Subjects: Devil (Resisting The) /Pride/Satan
Scripture Reference: Jas. 4: 7

On one occasion, Smith Wigglesworth was retiring for the night when his entire house began to shake. The shutters were banging and everything in the house was making a racket. He climbed back out of bed and lit his candle so he could investigate. When he stepped into the foyer, he looked and saw Satan himself, all reared back and sitting in the corner chair looking like a king. When Wigglesworth saw him, he said: "Oh, it's only you." Then, he blew out his candle and went back to bed. He treated Satan as though he was less than a lump of coal.

Always remember, Satan is king of nothing, unless YOU make him king of something.

Cleaning others

Subjects: Confidence/Evangelism/Righteousness/
Salvation/Victory
Scripture Reference: Phil. 1: 6

Jesus, like all good fisherman, catches the fish before attempting to clean it.

Becoming a Christian is not making a commitment to stop sinning and to "clean up our act." All we need to do is let Jesus catch us–He can handle the cleaning. The Lord assures us of this in His Word: "Being confident of this very thing, that He which hath begun a good work in you will perform it until the day of Jesus Christ:" Philippians 1:6

Not always friends

Subjects: Alcohol/Circumstances/Comfort/Drugs/
Enemies/Feelings/Friends/Safety/Trouble
Scripture Reference: Mt. 7: 15

A bird was flying through the air, having a beautiful time. Suddenly, however, he fell to the earth and landed in the middle of a cow pasture. No matter what he did, he could not seem to fly and it looked as though he was destined to lay there and die. He was wet and freezing and his situation was very bleak.

He started calling out for help: "Help me, help me, somebody help me!" Over and over he kept crying out for help. A nearby cow heard his cries and went to him to see if she could help the little bird. Of course, the cow could not pick the little bird up and carry it to a place of shelter and did not know what to do to help. After the cow pondered the situation she thought to herself: "All I can do is back up and drop a chip on the little bird. At least that way, it will be warm and safe." So she did. The bird was warm and safe and seemingly out of any immediate danger. However, the bird started thinking about all of this and was not happy about his situation. He started calling out again: "Help me, help me, somebody help me."

This time, a wolf heard his cries, went to him, dug him out of the cow chip, killed him and ate him.

The moral of this story is quite evident. Those who seem to bury you up to your neck in dung may not always be your enemies and those who dig you out may not always be your friends.

There can be many examples of the application of this story but the best seems to be drugs and alcohol. A person may be up to their neck in family problems, employment problems, school problems, etc. Then, someone (seemingly a friend) comes by and offers them alcohol or drugs. In the end, they realize that they are in worse condition now than before—that this person was not a friend at all.

Radiant resignation

**Subjects: Circumstances/Comfort/Healing/Joy/
Miracles/Peace/Will (God's)**
Scripture Reference: Rom. 8: 28 & Rom. 8: 38-39

After experiencing a marvelous healing in my own life, I watched one of my best friends die. I began to wonder why God heals some and not others. One day, while sitting at my desk, I picked up an article about healing and started reading it. This article proved to resolve my questions.

The article stated that a priest in the inner city had a tremendous healing ministry. People were coming to him from all over the country requesting that he lay hands on them and pray for them to receive a physical healing.

The news of his gift spread rapidly and several reporters went to interview him. One of the reporters asked the priest: "What is the greatest miracle you have witnessed?" The priest pondered the question for a moment and responded: "The greatest miracle I have witnessed is the radiant resignation in the faces of those turned away unhealed."

Coming to a place where we are resigned to God's perfect plan for our life causes us to radiate with His love, joy, and peace. Just knowing that we are in the palm of His hand and in His perfect will is greater than any physical healing we could ever receive.

The whole story

Subjects: Calvary/Eternal Life/Evangelism/Gospel/
**   Jesus/Witnessing**
Scripture Reference: Mt. 28: 19-20 & Acts 22: 15

A young boy, dressed in rags, stood looking in the front window of Macy's Department Store. He gazed intently at a portrait of the crucifix. A stranger stood beside him and as they stood in silence, looking at this moving portrait of Christ, suffering on the cross, the young boy said "That's Jesus. " Some soldiers nailed him to that cross." The stranger stood silently. Again the boy spoke, "He died there that day, and they took him away and buried him in a rich man's tomb." With that, the stranger hung his head, turned and walked slowly down the street. He was about a block away when the young boy came running after him, shouting: "Mister! Oh mister, I forgot to tell you, He arose from the dead and now He is alive forever!"

As Christians, it is our responsibility to tell the whole story, not just parts of it. Also, it is our responsibility to, joyfully; tell the story at every opportunity.

Circumstances

**Subjects: Attitude/Circumstances/Contentment/
       Happiness**
Scripture Reference: Prov. 16: 20 & Phil. 4: 11-13

Two men looked out from prison bars, one man looked down and saw the mud, the other looked up and saw the stars.

Two men looked out from mansions high, one looked down to see the mud and the other looked up to see the stars.

Sometimes our circumstances are great and everything seems to be going our way. Other times, our circumstances are poor and everything seems to be going wrong. It matters not! We still choose whether we are going to look up and search for the positive in our circumstances or if we are going to look down and search for the negative.

Wherever a person finds himself on the ladder of circumstances, he or she remains an "up-looker" or a "down-looker." A down-looker can have his circumstances any way he chooses and still not be happy. Being happy is exercising ones' ability to find happiness regardless of circumstances. Happiness is all around you and it has little to do with circumstances. The song says it all, "Happiness is the Lord."

Many individuals work very hard looking for things to be unhappy about—looking down. Actually, it takes less effort to look up and bask in happiness. Remember, pigs cannot look up, just down. We are not pigs, we are God's children, created in His image and for His purpose.

Friendship

Subjects: Attitude/Circumstances/Friendship/Prayer/
       Thankfulness
Scripture Reference: Col. 3: 15 & I Thess. 5: 18

Albert C. Outler, a famous author, shared some precious
memories about his childhood which I always found
encouraging. He said that he grew up in the Virginia's during a
time when most parents had a "nanny" to help with the rearing
of the children.

His nanny's name was Anna Maria Sophia Virginia Avalon
Thessalonians. She allowed him and her other friends to simply
call her Anna. For that, he was quite thankful.

He said that before she would eat, she would always bow her
head and say "Thank you Lord for these vittles." One day,
young Outler asked her "Anna, what's vittles?" She said:
"Why, that's what you have to eat." He told her that he did
not understand why she always thanked the Lord for what she
had to eat–that she would have it to eat whether she thanked
the Lord or not. She simply smiled and said: "Yea, but it makes
everything taste better."

She taught Albert a lot about the Lord and helped him to
understand Christian values. She especially taught him how to
be thankful. She explained that being thankful was a game that
"an old colored preacher" taught her to play. She said: "It's
fun to look for things to be thankful for. Take this morning for
instance. I laid in bed all lazy like wondering what in the world

do I have to be thankful for? Then, from the kitchen came the fresh smell of coffee. I just looked up to Heaven and said thank you Lord for coffee and thank you for the smell of it!"

He grew up and left home and became a successful writer and teacher. One day, he was called home to Anna's dying bedside. He said that her body was twisted with crippling arthritis and he could hardly recognize her as she lay in her bed of pain.

Mr. Outler could not help but wonder what in the world Anna could ever be thankful for now. How could a person be thankful about anything when they are in this condition? Just then, she looked at him and, with her last breath, said: "Thank you Lord for such fine friends."

Being content

Subjects: Circumstances/Contentment/Prayer/
Will (God's)/Works
Scripture Reference: Eph. 6: 6 & Jas. 4: 15

Mother Teresa's primary prayer remained the same throughout her life. It was: "Lord, just let me be your rubber ball."

Mother Teresa recognized that sometimes a child wants to take the rubber ball out of the toy box and play with it. Other times, a child is content to just know that the rubber ball is there, safely tucked away and ready at the child's beckoning. She understood that the Lord may have her actively involved in a much needed ministry. Or, if He choose, He could just keep her up underneath His everlasting wing, ready should He need her for service. It was His choice whether to use her or not. Her responsibility was to be ready for service and content whether she was in a state of active ministry or being held in a time of refreshing and renewal.

For years, though she was well-equipped and well-versed, my own mother confessed that the Lord was keeping her to Himself like a "bird in a cage." He would not even let her teach Sunday school class. Nevertheless, her prayer remained the same, "God, I just want to be in your perfect will." Her primary ministry was not to the community or to the Body of Christ, it was to her own family. She was our private theologian and God's rubber ball.

A profound essay

Subjects: Meditation/Miracles/Prayer/Wisdom (Divine)/Worship
Scripture Reference: I Tim. 4: 15

A young man, who was attending seminary, was struggling financially and he really needed some divine help. A notice was posted on the school's bulletin board indicating that an essay contest was scheduled for the following Saturday morning. The winner would receive $1,000.

At 9:00 a.m. the following Saturday morning, this young man, along with about one hundred other students, met at the school to hear the contest rules. They would have exactly one hour to write an essay on the subject of Jesus' first miracle of turning water into wine. All the students were provided with stacks of plain white paper and plenty of pens and pencils. Then, they were told to begin.

As he looked around the room he noticed that everyone was writing feverishly. However, his mind seemed to go blank. He needed the money very much but he just could not address the subject. He just sat there and prayed and meditated about this wonderful miracle.

Before he realized it, fifty-five minutes had passed and he heard the professor announce that they had five minutes in order to complete the essay. All of the other contest participants had stacks of pages which they had written. He, on the other hand, had only blank sheets. He had not written the first word. Moments before the contest concluded, he wrote one sentence and placed his essay on the desk with the others. He was totally exhausted from his time of meditation and worship so he went home and collapsed across his bed. He was despondent because he failed so miserably.

The following Monday, the winner of the essay contest was announced and it was him. Even though his essay was only one sentence long, it was the most profound essay of all. He wrote: "The water looked at its Creator and blushed."

Manipulation through guilt

Subjects: Control/Guilt/Manipulation/Shame
Scripture Reference: Prov. 14: 35 & Prov. 15: 1-2

What is a "good Jewish mother?" Well, it is not a Jew or even a mother. It is a term applied to any individual who uses shame and guilt as a means of manipulation.

Some people are excellent at it and have fine tuned it into an art. It usually sounds something like this: "No, no. You go right ahead and enjoy yourself. I'll be just fine here all alone. If anything bad happens to me, I don't want you to feel ashamed or guilty." Or, perhaps: "I haven't heard from you for awhile, I guess you don't have time for me. That's okay, I understand. I have lots of things to do to occupy my time–even though the television is broken and my arthritis keeps me from working in the garden. I'm okay. I don't expect you to spend your valuable time calling me or stopping by."

Do you use shame and guilt to manipulate others? Is someone using shame and guilt to manipulate you?

Not by might

Subjects: Control/Faith/Self-reliance/Trust
Scripture Reference: Zech. 4: 6b

A young man was excited about his first lesson to qualify for his private license as an airplane pilot. After he and his instructor were safely in the air, the instructor told him to take the controls which he was eager to do.

Under his control, the airplane was weaving from side to side and up and down. He was literally all over the sky. The instructor looked at his hands which were tightly on the controls–so tight that his knuckles were white. Then, to his amazement, the instructor told him to place his hands in his lap. When he did, the plane leveled right out. The instructor said: "Son, the first thing you need to learn is that this airplane can fly. You do not have to hold it in the air by your own might and by your own will power–it can fly!" Recall the Word: "...Not by might, nor by power, but by my Spirit, saith the Lord of hosts." Zec. 4: 6b

God has the whole world in His hands and this includes you and me. We need to learn to take our hands off the steering wheel of our lives and put our trust and faith in the Lord. He will guide us "by His Spirit." When we take control, all we do is get in His way and mess everything up.

Need for authority

Subjects: Authority/Obedience/Submission
Scripture Reference: Col. 3: 18-22

I saw a bumper sticker the other day that read: "Question authority!" That seems to be the trend that the world is taking. Sometimes when I see parents with their children in public, I have a difficult time telling which one is the parent. For the most part, the children are the parents. The children command and the adults obey. Children are now being taught that they have the right to question, even challenge their parent's decisions. Authority is absurd and cruel–that is the popular opinion!

I read an article in a magazine regarding the need for authority and it helped me to understand just how important submitting to authority can be. The U.S. Navy was giving serious consideration to easing up on the whole issue regarding authority.

Many individuals believed that the entire matter was simply unnecessary and that every sailor should be given more equal rights. The move was towards allowing, even the lowest ranking sailors, to give input (their opinion), to question superior officers and the decisions that were being made.

During all of the debate an elderly, retired naval officer wrote a letter to the Naval Command Headquarters in favor of maintaining absolute authority within the Navy and all departments of the military. In his letter he told about an incident on a gun ship. Five seamen were cleaning one of the large guns on the deck as a Naval officer stood on the deck just above them and watched. Suddenly, the cable that held the large gun in place snapped. The five seaman could not see it from where they were but the officer, looking down from above, saw it clearly.

In a split second the officer yelled "DOWN!" Without hesitation or delay, all five seamen hit the deck. The steel cable came around the gun like a whip. If the seaman had not immediately obeyed the officer, they would have all been killed instantly. When they heard his command, they did not fold their arms over their chest, turn to him and say: "Why?" They were taught to obey authority so when he yelled "down," they did what they were told to do—they went down.

Is authority important? Authority, although it should never be abused, is absolutely essential; lives may depend on it. Sometimes we wonder why God does certain things or allows certain things to happen to us. He is our final authority and He requires obedience. We are not equal partners with Him. He is the Creator and we are the created. We need to remember this. Questioning Him will lead us into serious trouble, but giving Him a place of absolute authority over our lives will save us. He loves us far more than we love ourselves.

God's plan and will

Subjects: Death/Destiny/Miracles/Will (God's)
Scripture Reference: Ps. 103: 14-17; Ps. 139: 16
& Rom. 8: 28

When I was attending summer classes at Duke University's School of Divinity, I was faced with a question that I could not answer. We just returned from a long Fourth of July weekend when our class was called to order. One of the divinity students asked the professor if he could share the story of a miracle that took place in his hometown in central Virginia over the holiday. The professor assured him that he would be delighted to hear about the miracle. With that, the entire class enthusiastically agreed.

He stated that a train was racing down the track at about eighty miles an hour. Suddenly, the emergency cord was pulled and all of the alarms in the engine area started sounding. The engineer knew that there must be an emergency and that he was being signaled to stop the train as fast as he could. He hit the brakes with everything the train had and it finally came to a stop right in a curve. The conductor, the only other person on the train, came forward and asked the engineer why he stopped so abruptly.

The engineer told him that it was because he had pulled the emergency cord. The conductor denied being anywhere near it. They were both puzzled by the incident but decided to continue their journey. The train's speed was only about five miles an hour as they rounded out the curve. There, right in the middle of the track, was a five or six year old boy with his foot stuck in the track. Had they not stopped just as they entered the curve, they could never have stopped by the time they would have seen him—not at eighty miles an hour!

The entire class applauded jubilantly! What a wonderful miracle. With that, however, the professor asked the class a question. "Who pulled the cord?" God! We all answered. Everyone in the class agreed that it was God who reached down from Heaven and pulled the emergency cord to stop the train just in time to save the little boy's life.

Then, silence came over the class when the professor asked: "What are you going to tell the parents of the child who is hit by a train and killed? Where was God for their little child? Doesn't God love their little child as much as this one? Was He too busy to reach down from Heaven and pull the cord and stop the train for their child?"

After much debate, we all agreed that there is only one answer. God has a perfect plan for each of us. Some complete their journey and fulfill their purpose before others. "All things work together for good to them that love God, to them who are the called according to His purpose." Romans 8:28

God's will

Subjects: Control/Omnipotent/Will (God's)
Scripture Reference: Mk. 10: 27

One of the biggest questions that is raised in a good philosophy and religion class is this: "Can your God do anything?" When the question is raised, the class normally responds with an emphatic YES! He is omnipotent! The professor continues: "Can your God create a rock so big that He cannot move it?"

At that point you can cut the silence with a knife. What a paradox! If the class holds their ground and insists that their God can do anything including creating a rock that big, then the professor simply says: "There is something your God can't do—move that rock He just created."

The answer is actually quite simple. God has surrounded Himself with a wall that He will not cross. The wall is His "will" and He will not go outside it. Can He do something that is against His will? Absolutely! However, He Will not!

In addition, He WILL NOT remember past sins that were confessed and washed away by the blood of the Lamb–Jesus.

Hoping for wisdom

Subjects: Humility/Knowledge/Wisdom (Divine)
Scripture Reference: I Cor. 1: 27, 31b

After a young man completed medical school he had to appear before the medical board for an oral interview. Receiving his medical license depended solely upon this review. A very old medical doctor, who was a member of the review board, was given the responsibility to question the young applicant.

The old man happened to be a very dear friend of the young man's father. Many wondered if he would be unreasonably severe in order to overcompensate for the personal friendship. However, he was quite fair. He asked the applicant: "What are wisdom teeth?" The young doctor gave a complete medical report regarding wisdom teeth and his report was quite proficient. He concluded his report by stating that wisdom teeth normally come later than all the other teeth, for some, when they are in their twenties. This, he said, is why they are called wisdom teeth–because one is thought to be a little wiser by the age they appear. Then, the old man looked at him and asked: "Sir, do you have wisdom teeth?" To this, the young man responded: "No sir, but I hope to someday."

I, like the young doctor, "hope to someday." I know, however, that if I ever receive wisdom and if that wisdom has any value, it will come from the Lord, not from man.

> *The Word says: "But God hath chosen the foolish things of the world to confound the wise; and God hath chosen the weak things of the world to confound the things which are mighty;.... He that glorieth, let him glory in the Lord."*
> *I Co. 1:27, 31b*

Quoting Aristotle

Subjects: Anger/Change
Scripture Reference: Prov. 16: 32 & Eccl. 7: 9

Aristotle said: "Anybody can become angry; that is easy, but to become angry at the right person and right degree for the right purpose at the right time in the right way, is not easy."

There is something called righteous anger. It does not involve self. It is an anger that arises from injustice done to others and it always demands change. The anger produces energy and the energy is used to bring about that change.

Quoting Chesterdon

Subjects: Forgiveness/Love/Pardon
Scripture Reference: Mt. 5: 44, 46

Chesterdon said: "If love cannot love the un-lovely, then love is no virtue at all. If   pardon cannot pardon the unpardonable, then pardon is no virtue at all. And, if forgiveness cannot forgive the unforgivable, then forgiveness is no virtue at all."

Quoting John Wesley

Subjects: Fellowship/Worship
Scripture Reference: Jn. 4: 24

John Wesley said: "You are not an audience come to hear a sermon. WE are the family of God, gathered about the Father's table in fellowship with Him and with one another."

It's not a garden

Subjects: Discipline/Effecting Change/Guidance
**   (Children) /Parenting/Responsibility**
Scripture Reference: Prov. 22: 6

A widower dating a widow, who was about the same age, invited her to his apartment one evening after a pleasant dinner out.

As they sat on the sofa after drinking their evening cup of coffee, he announced that it was time for him to take her home. She asked him why he wanted to take her home so early and he explained that it was because: "Tomorrow is Sunday and I want to take my son Johnny to church so he can learn about Jesus." Johnny was about twelve years old and she had a little boy the same age. She told him that she did not attend church and did not want to raise her son in the church to be influenced by the Gospel of Jesus Christ.

The man was stunned by her remark. He knew that she was a believer and could not imagine rearing a child outside of the church environment. The lady explained that, yes, she believed in Jesus Christ, however, she wanted her son to decide for himself. She explained that if she took her son to church, he would merely be indoctrinated and that it would be too biased. She wanted him to review the entire matter of Christ's resurrection when he was older and to decide for himself without having been "forced" into the faith by attending Sunday school and church. He did not say anything more about the matter. He simply brought her jacket and took her home.

The next Saturday night he invited her to his home again. This time, while they were having their coffee, he asked if she would like to see his flower garden. She was elated with the idea stating that she would be "thrilled to see it." He escorted her through a set of sliding glass doors that led to an outdoor patio.

There were four large sections blocked off for a flower garden, two on either side of the walkway. However, the entire area was overgrown with weeds. She could not help but laugh and say: "This is not a flower garden! This is just a patch of weeds!"

He explained that a couple of years ago, he had the entire patio sectioned off and filled it with top soil and fertilizer and let it grow whatever it wanted. He was hoping for flowers but the garden area decided to grow weeds. As gently as she could, she explained that the ground does not naturally grow flowers, that it only grows weeds. She told him that if he wants flowers, he has to plant and cultivate them. To this, he responded: "What time do you want me to pick you and Tommy up for church tomorrow?"

Children will not end up as responsible, God-fearing adults who are a blessing to society and to the Kingdom of God unless they are cultivated and taught the wonderful truths found in the Holy Scriptures. Evil does not have to be cultivated anymore than weeds. Godliness and goodness, like flowers, must be planted and nurtured.

The dressing room

**Subjects: Comfort/Death/Eternal Life/Heaven
Scripture Reference: Rom. 8: 28-29**

During the funeral of a young child, the minister stated the following:

> *"Life is like a dressing room where we dress and
> prepare to meet our Creator. Some, like this little
> child, dress faster than others."*

Turning the other cheek!

Topics: Enemies/Forgiveness
Scripture Reference: Mt. 5: 39

Forgiveness is the scent of the rose on the heel that crushed it.

Puff Graham!

Topics: Favor (Divine)/Humility/Prayer
Scripture Reference: Zech. 4: 6b & Lk. 14: 11

How did The Reverend Billy Graham become so famous—a minister whose name is known by nearly everyone on Earth? You would never have guessed! Let me relay the story as best I can remember.

He was preaching a revival at a very small church and only a few people were in attendance. A couple of little old ladies thought he was pretty good and they decided to pray for him and for the revival. One of them came up with a great idea! She thought it would be great if the revival could be announced in their city's newspaper. Naively, she picked up the telephone and dialed the number of one of the largest newspaper organizations in the world—the one owned by William Randolph Hearst.

A phone began to ring out in the main secretarial section of the building. It was a large room with desks lined everywhere. The phone just rang and rang and no one was there to answer it. As it was ringing, Mr. Hearst walked by, and the constant ringing aggravated him to no end. In total anger and disgust, he picked up the phone and said: "What do you want!"

The little old lady (who may have been scared out of her wits) explained that they were having a revival at their church and that they had a wonderful preacher but that they needed to get the word out so more people would come. He growled back at her saying something like: "And just exactly why should we help?" To that she responded by saying: "Because it is what our city needs." He said: "Hogwash" and hung up the phone on her.

Mr. Hearst took about four steps, turned around and went back to the phone and picked it up to engage the newspaper's operator. Here is what he said to the operator: "Telegraph all editors with: 'Puff Graham, signed Hearst'."

The telegram went out to every editor of every affiliated newspaper in the country. You cannot even begin to imagine how fearful everyone was because they did not have a clue as to what William Randolph Hearst was ordering them to do. Who was Graham? They, by some miracle, figured it out and that evening there were so many newspaper reporters at that little church that one could hardly find a seat. The next day just about every newspaper in the country led with front page stories talking about Billy Graham and how he was bringing hope back to the country.

Jesus is not the "only" way!

Topics: Grace/Mercy/Perfection/Salvation/Sin
Scripture Reference: Jn. 14: 6 & Rom. 3: 23-26

Jesus is not the only way to Heaven! When I heard the late Dr. D. James Kennedy say that, I nearly fell out of my chair! My antennae went up and my ears shut out every sound except the sound of his voice. I needed to hear his explanation for such an outrageous statement!

Needless to say, I was delighted with his follow-up. He said (paraphrased):

> *"Anyone can go to Heaven and, no, you do not have to have a savior, you just need to be perfect—without sin. If you are without sin, you will have a place reserved for you in Heaven.*
>
> *However, if you have ever sinned, you are in trouble and you need a savior—someone who has never sinned, someone who is perfect. So far, there is only one who qualifies—His name is Jesus.*
>
> *He offers you His mercy and grace—an opportunity to go to Heaven through Him, even though you have sinned. Do you need a Savior?"*

Attention!

Topics: **Criticism/Persecution/Suffering**
Scripture Reference: **Mt. 5: 10, Mt. 24: 9 & 2 Tim. 3: 12**

A whale doesn't get harpooned until it spouts! When you start spouting—especially if you are spouting off for Jesus, get ready for the harpoons! It's okay though—He who is in you is greater than he who is in the world.

The Law of Reciprocity

Topics: **Giving/Law (God's)/Obedience/Tithing**
Scripture Reference: **Lev. 27: 30, Mal. 3: 10 & 2 Cor. 9: 7**

Pat Robertson told a story that had a tremendous impact on me—one that helped me to understand how blessed we are when we tithe—not that we tithe in order to be blessed!

He said that the Lord sent a missionary to a poor, small village in Africa. He faithfully proclaimed the Word to everyone who would listen and he taught them all the Biblical principles: forgiveness, faith, and mercy, he spoke on all of them. Then he prayed to the Lord asking if he could go home since his work was completed. However, the Lord said to him, your work is not done, you have not taught them ALL my principles, you have not taught them to tithe. The missionary said: "Lord! These people are very poor! Surely you would not want me to encourage them to give! Would you?"

The Lord told him that he could not go home until he taught them about tithing, so, the following Sunday, during the worship service, reluctantly, he explained the principle of tithing and how the first fruits are to go to the Lord.

The following Sunday and every Sunday thereafter, they came bringing their first fruits—perhaps just an egg or a baby chick—whatever they could from whatever they had. Faithfully, every one of them practiced tithing, not begrudgingly, but with cheerful hearts!

Pat concluded by explaining that a few years later, a drought hit the entire region and everyone lost all their crops—everyone except the tithing members of this Christian church. Every single one of them flourished and everything they did was blessed by the Lord. Of course, it must be stated over and over again that one must never, ever tithe in order to gain or receive blessings. We tithe because we are obedient servants, what the Lord does as a result is entirely up to Him. He owes us nothing and He is certainly not indebted to us because we are obedient and tithe.

Dr. Richard G. Arno

PART THREE

PERSONAL EXPERIENCES

During my ministry, I have experienced many things, from spiritual visions during my times of meditation to actual events wherein I believe that the Lord spoke very clearly to me.

Being alone with the Lord, to just meditate and become lost in His glory, is something that I consider to be quite precious. It is during these special times that He teaches me and gives me wisdom. These lessons usually come as visions and I must admit that they are above and beyond me. That is to say, none of them, not one single one, can be attributed to me, they are divinely inspired.

Prayerfully, these accounts will deepen your faith, broaden your spiritual horizons and bless you as you grow in your relationship with our Heavenly Father.

Turnpike turn around

Subjects: Call (Divine)/Commitment/Destiny/
Direction(Divine)/Misperception/
Salvation/Service
Scripture Reference: Mt. 16: 26

When I was twelve years old, I went forward during a Sunday morning church service, knelt at the altar and received the Lord as my personal Savior. From that moment on, I have always loved to sing the song: "Lord, I want to be a Christian in my Heart."

I did want to be a Christian. However, for me, it seemed to be much more than that. I could not just be a Christian and choose some wonderful career. For me, being a Christian coincided with answering God's call on my life for full-time ministry. A call which I resented and resisted.

By the time I was seventeen years old, I graduated from high school and entered the army. By the time I was nineteen I was a Sergeant and felt that the world was my oyster. Surely God had forgotten about the call on my life and would let me alone and let me make my mark. Not true. In fact, He would not leave me alone. Everything I touched fell apart and I was miserable, not in success, in failure. He just did not want me to succeed at anything I attempted. Perhaps He knew that if I was able to succeed, I would deny Him all the more.

While traveling from Philadelphia to Pittsburgh along the Pennsylvania Turnpike, I had a spiritual experience much like the one I had when I was twelve. However, by this time, I was twenty-four years old, an accountant and on my way to audit a large retail outlet.

I was making good money but everything seemed to cost me ten times more than it cost anyone else. The more I advanced, the more I fell behind. Speeding down the highway in a hurry to go nowhere, the Lord began to minister to me.

He asked me where I was going and I told him "to my grave as fast as I can get there!" Then, He asked me what I was accomplishing with my life on my way to the grave. What an absurd question! I was accomplishing a lot! I was catching people stealing money and encouraging their employers to prosecute. Nevertheless, the response that came out of my mouth was different from the one I was thinking. I simply said: "Nothing." He showed me a grave with a body inside and all the person's worldly possessions stacked around the grave side.

The Lord showed me that when I die, nothing I obtained during my life would have any value—that these possessions would simply be passed on to my heirs to be squandered. He helped me to understand that the greatest inheritance I could provide my children would be knowledge of Him in the hopes of their eternal salvation. No man could leave a greater legacy or inheritance than to teach his children about Jesus. He also showed me the importance of accomplishments and values.

I envisioned a young man in high school who only had one goal in life—to design and build the greatest building on earth. His entire life was dedicated to this mission. After high school he attended college to become an architect and continued his commitment to this single goal. He did not participate in any family or social activities. He had no relationships and was not involved with anything which would distract him from his work.

Towards the end of his life, when he was an old man, he saw his dream come true. The building he spent his entire life designing was completed and I witnessed the cutting of the ribbon and the grand opening. It was, indeed, the greatest building on earth. Then, I saw the architect's headstone. Above it, I saw the pages of a calendar flashing. I saw years pass like minutes, one thousand in all. Suddenly, I found myself standing outside of the marvelous building which, through time, turned to rubble.

With this, the Lord spoke to my heart. He said that the things that we accomplish on earth will all pass away, but the things we do for Him will last eternally. He asked me if I wanted to waste my life or if I wanted to make an eternal difference. I took the next exit off the turnpike and returned home to enter the ministry.

All wrapped up

Topics: Grace/New (Being Made)/Renewal
Scripture Reference: Ps. 51: 10 & Lam. 5: 21

Our youngest son, Jaysen, shared a wonderful story with me one time and it was very enlightening. He explained that he was traveling on Route 17 in North Carolina and was "in the middle of nowhere" when he realized he was nearly out of gas. Like many of us, he began to pray for a miracle and God blessed him. He found a station and filled up his gas tank.

However, when he went inside to pay with his credit card, he was devastated when it was rejected over and over.

The attendant asked for the card again and this time, he wrapped it up in a piece of plastic. Once more, he slid the card through the machine, but now it worked! Jaysen asked him what happened and he said: "Son, sometimes they get all scratched up, scraped and marred, but if you wrap them up in something clean, they work like new."

Wow! That is exactly what happens to us! We get all scratched up, scraped and marred. We are bruised and basically thrown away (if only by ourselves) and then God wraps us up in the garment of Jesus and makes us whole again. Then, when the Father looks at us, He sees the beauty of His son, Jesus, and we are like new.

A struggle within

Subjects: Call (Divine)/Confidence/Destiny/Direction (Divine)/Doubt/Fact/Humility / Misunderstanding/Obstacles/ Self-exhultation/Service
Scripture Reference: I Cor. 1: 26-27

I believe that all individuals who feel that God has a divine call on their lives have to go through a time of questioning and a deep inner searching. Am I really called into the ministry or is this something that I want—something that I birthed in my own heart? Is this really God or just me?

I struggled with this question for months on end. On one occasion, I believe that the Lord spoke to me and the question was settled forever. The Lord asked me if going into the ministry was my desire. My answer was emphatically "yes." Then, another question came. Who placed the desire in your heart? Are you (Richard Arno) so great that you could accomplish such a mission–birth such a sacred desire?

How humbling! I knew immediately that the desire that burned in my heart was placed there by Him. That is how He calls us! He calls us through the desires of our heart. He plants the desire and then waters it with His love.

A selfish man

Subjects: Attitude/Giving/Humility/Pride/
Selfishness/Thankfulness
Scripture Reference: Col. 3: 12

The death of a child, no matter their age, must be the most difficult thing for a parent to experience. It is also difficult for the family's pastor because the parents are looking to the pastor for answers–answers that are often not a pastor's to give.

One family, which was quite active in our church, was very excited because their son was coming home from college over the Labor Day weekend. Their excitement turned to despair when they learned that on his way home, he fell asleep behind the wheel and was killed instantly. His car left the highway and went into a deep concrete culvert.

The Lord used me to help the family through this terrible tragedy. We had a lovely service in the church and at the grave side.

While walking with the parents back to the car after the grave side service concluded, the boy's father shook my hand to thank me for all the help I had provided during their time of grief. Something was balled up in the palm of his hand which he transferred to my hand. I looked down to see that it was a ten dollar bill. When I saw it, I said: "Danny, I don't want this money and I am not going to take it." With that, I attempted to force it back on to him.

He looked in my eyes and said: "Rev. Arno, you are a very selfish man!" Selfish? What did he mean selfish? I was refusing $10. That seemed generous to me!

He explained that I was cheating him out of the only way he had to show his appreciation. Then, I realized that my refusal was an expression of my own pride. He needed to give me something and I needed to swallow my pride and accept it with humility and gratitude.

There is a time to give and there is a time to receive. Of the two, receiving is the hardest.

If God is for you

Subjects: Comfort/Confidence/Direction(Divine)/
Obedience/Omnipotent/Will (God's)
Scripture Reference: Ex. 19: 5 & Prov. 16: 7

Shortly after I accepted the Lord's call on my life to go into the ministry, I was faced with many obstacles.

I was a member of a Methodist Church (now United Methodist) and was fairly active. I thought I had an excellent relationship with my pastor; however, I was very mistaken. When I went to his office and sat down in front of his desk, I told him that I decided to go into the ministry. I honestly expected him to congratulate me and to pledge his support. Instead, he leaned back in his chair and said: "Richard Arno has decided to go into the ministry! Walla, walla, walla." He even included the rolling of his hands and arms. I was devastated.

He finally agreed to talk to the District Superintendent to see if the Board of Ministry would meet with me. After a few days, I received a call from the District Superintendent. He told me that he did not think he could do anything to help me and that they really had little need for an uneducated man like myself.

It was a beautiful day and I went for a walk down by the pond behind our house. As I walked, I explained my situation to God. I told Him that I had absolutely no support and that everyone seemed to be against me. I thanked Him for the call on my life. However, I told Him that He would have to release me from the call since it would be impossible to overcome the obstacles. I honestly felt a sense of relief; after all, it was not my fault that I could not obey Him. As I left the pond and walked back towards the house, He stopped me in my tracks.

If I ever heard the Lord's voice in my life, I know in my heart that I heard it right then. The still small voice said: "I am God, Creator of all things, if I am for you, who can be against you?"

When I heard these words, I was filled with new enthusiasm, encouragement and determination. I knew that God was going to make a way for me. Within the hour, the District Superintendent called me back and told me that he had changed his mind–that he did want to help me. I was approved to start school immediately. Within six months of that day, I was appointed as a student pastor of two small Methodist Churches.

Scales in the sky

**Subjects: Death/Destiny/Faith/Forgiveness/Grace/
                    Heaven/Hope/Jesus/Mercy**
Scripture Reference: Dan. 5: 27 & Rom. 3: 23-26

During my morning devotions, when I was in my mid to late twenties, I envisioned myself soaring through space. In the far distance I saw what appeared to be huge scales, much like those you would see carved on the front of a courthouse.

I was heading straight for them and they grew larger and larger. Suddenly, I stopped right in front of them. I was told that I had to weigh perfect before I could enter into heaven. I knew in my heart that I could never weigh perfect. I was cluttered with debris and clothed in heavy garments of filth.

As I stood there in utter hopelessness, the Lord Jesus Christ stepped up to my side and, in my heart, I heard him say: "I will stand on the scales for you—you can go around them."

I knew in that moment that my only hope of ever entering Heaven would be Jesus. I have no other hope.

Love the people

**Subjects: Caring/Confidence/Love/Priorities/
  Responsibility/ Success
Scripture Reference: 1 Cor. 13 (NKJV)**

About a year after I entered the ministry, I began to get discouraged. I was facing a minimum of eight years of college and trying to pastor two churches. In addition to being a college student, husband and father, I was expected to preach, teach, visit, perform weddings, conduct funerals, provide administrative leadership for the church, conduct board meetings and participate in conference activities. To be perfectly honest with you, I became overwhelmed with a sense of fear that I could not succeed at all of this; that I would FAIL. I decided to drive up to Weston, West Virginia, and talk to my District Superintendent, Rev. Billy Scott Mick.

As always, he welcomed me and made me feel very comfortable to share anything I needed to talk to him about. As we sat together, I began to list all of my responsibilities. I remember saying, "Rev. Mick, I am scared that I cannot do it all. I am scared that I will fail."

As he sat there and smiled, he said, "Well Dick, would you like to have the keys to success?" The keys to success? What do you mean, the keys to success? I was overwhelmed with a sense of excitement that this man could give me an absolute, foolproof, step-by-step way to guarantee my success in the ministry.

Rev. Mick went on to explain that there are three "keys to success" that are available to any and all ministers. These three keys would ensure that no one would ever fail in the ministry, even me. He asked me again if I would like to have the three keys. "YES! What are the keys to success?" He smiled again, leaned back in his chair and said, "First, LOVE YOUR PEOPLE; second, LOVE YOUR PEOPLE; and third, LOVE YOUR PEOPLE."

How simple, yet profound and true. If a minister genuinely loves his people from his heart, he will never fail, no matter how badly he preaches, fails to show up for his meetings or forgets the baby's name during dedication, he will not fail.

These keys to success do not only apply to the ministry. They apply to the school system, medical field, business and in the home. God's command to love applies to everyone.

Trusting the Lord

Topics: Fear/Surrender/Trust
Scripture Reference: Ps. 20: 7

In the summer of 2001 we were experiencing something strange on the east coast of the United States. There were several shark attacks, both in the Atlantic and the Gulf of Mexico. In fact, there were so many attacks that year, that it is commonly referred to now as "the summer of the sharks."

That year, our youngest son, Jaysen, was visiting us from his home state of North Carolina. He and I were fishing from a pier in Sarasota Bay and it was dark. Dusk and early evening hours are common times for shark attacks—times when one should not be in the water.

Suddenly, he dropped one of my favorite rods off the dock and into the murky waters. Without a thought, he jumped in after it. I was petrified! He dived down and found the rod the very first time. That in itself was amazing.

Neither one of us realized it but the tide was low, and when he tried to climb back onto the pier, it was too high and he could not make it. He was bobbing in the darkness and being shredded by the barnacles; not a good situation during the "summer of the sharks." I had a good clasp on his wrist, but with all of my strength, I could not pull him up to safety. Over and over he kept asking me to let him go so he could swim around the dock to the shore and I kept telling him no. "Let me go dad, I am being cut to pieces!" "No, I can't!" Finally, I realized that our only hope was for him to swim around so, with all of my trust in the Lord, I released him.

Jaysen swam way out around the docks which form a "T" that jut out into the Gulf– it was well over 100 yards. Before long, he was out of range and I could no longer see nor hear him. Then finally, I heard the beautiful sound of breaking water as he climbed the stairs to the dock's re-entry. Although bloody and tired, he was safe and, to say the least, I was relieved.

Several years passed and, one day, we were talking about the incident. He told me that for several months he remained "proud" of the courage he showed that night when retrieving my rod and reel. Then he said:

"Dad, the Lord convicted me of that. He showed me that my courage could not begin to compare with your courage. What courage you must have had to let me go into the darkness and to trust the Lord with my safety. What Jesus went through on Calvary was horrendous—beyond our comprehendsion, but Dad, what must it have been like for God to let His Son go into the darkness to endure the torture of Calvary?" Oh God, How great thou art!

Snow on hill

Subjects: Forgiveness/Goodness/Grace/Hope/
Mercy/Sin
Scripture Reference: Ps. 23: 6

During the late 60's I was the pastor of two small United Methodist Churches in a remote town located in central West Virginia. I often said that if it was snowing anywhere in the world, it was snowing in this town. Personally, I am a sunshine lover, yet snow represents one of the most beautiful spiritual experiences I ever had.

Our parsonage was located on a small hill that overlooked the town of Cowan, West Virginia. I normally started my morning by standing on the front porch and taking in some of the fresh mountain air. To my right was a much larger hill, and on the top of that hill stood a large water tower which was used by the town as its main water source.

Beneath the water tower, and all around it, was the town graveyard. Looking up to the graveyard, I would recall the many, many grave side services I had conducted up there, and the pain and suffering I had witnessed because of the loss of a dear loved one.

As I stood on the porch gazing up toward the hill, I often thought that it would be a beautiful spot to start my day. From up there, the sunrise would be spectacular. I could have my morning devotions alone, with just the Lord and His beautiful creation. It would even be more spectacular if I could be there before sunrise and after a fresh fallen snow.

This spiritual fantasy became a reality for me when one morning I awoke early, stepped outside and was confronted with a beautiful fresh snow fall. It was still dark and a perfect opportunity for me to "seize the moment." I rushed upstairs, threw on some heavy clothes, winter boots and grabbed my Bible and a flashlight.

It was extremely difficult making my way up the hill. The snow was much deeper than I first realized and I had to zigzag around the tombstones and be careful of my footing.

Without a doubt, it was a magnificent experience. As the sun began to rise, the morning light revealed the silhouette of the town below looking like a beautiful white paradise. My heart filled with joy recalling the words of the song: "He has the whole world in His hands." Not only does he care for the little tiny baby, but the mother whose little tiny baby may have been stillborn.

Making my way back down the steep hill I tried to stay within the path I had broken on my trip upward. I remember slipping and falling several times, getting back on my feet, sliding and falling again. "It was worth it," I kept saying to myself, "it was worth it!" When I arrived at the parsonage, I stood on the front porch and looked back toward the hill. I remember chuckling as I thought that no one would ever believe the town preacher was up on the hill that morning. It looked more like the town drunk had been there.

My spiritual experience was not over. In fact, the best was yet to come. I worked that day in my office, which was located inside the parsonage. Since it was too bad to travel, I had a perfect opportunity to make a few telephone calls, read some articles which were gathering dust on my desk and do those "special things" we all seem to put off.

The next morning when I awoke, it was daylight. After dressing, I walked out on to the front porch again. This time when I looked up toward the hill, I was surprised to see that my tracks from the day before were gone. It had snowed again during the night and all physical traces of my spiritual journey were gone. Just then, a Scripture was brought to my mind. It was Psalm 23: 6a: "Surely, goodness and mercy shall follow me all the days of my life:"

I was always aware of the fact that the Lord goes before us as we make our way through life. I even knew that He walks beside us; however, for the first time in my life, I realized that the Lord FOLLOWS US!

I saw first hand that the Lord follows us. Like a pure, wind-driven snow, the Lord follows behind us, straightening out all of the crooked tracks we leave. He follows us, purifying, straightening and re-working our blundering ways into something good and holy—something He can use for His Kingdom and His glory.

We all make serious mistakes and we all have our hidden sins—if not overt sins, then inverted sins of the spirit. We have doubts, judgmental attitudes and I am sure that there are many things about us which displease the Lord. Good news! His goodness and mercy follows us all the days of our lives!

Personal walk

Subjects: **Eternal life/Jesus/Priorities/Responsibility/
Understanding/Works**
Scripture Reference: Lk. 12: 47

On one occasion, I envisioned a steep hill and at the very top of the hill stood Jesus. Masses of people were making their way up the hill towards the Lord. I was about half way up when I started noticing the people around me. Many were beginning to faint and were weary from the journey. They were thirsty, hungry and very discouraged.

My compassion for the weary travelers became so great that I stopped and set up a place of rescue. I started helping people to their feet, giving them a refreshing drink of water and encouraging them to continue the climb–to fight the good fight–to finish the race.

Suddenly, the Lord rebuked me. He showed me that it was good for me to have compassion for the others and to assist them whenever and however I could. However, I was forbidden to stop moving ever towards Him for the sake of doing good and helping others. He made it very clear that my first responsibility was my own soul and my own personal journey.

For the first time in my life; I fully realized that good works are fine, but not a substitute for my personal relationship with Jesus.

Life is a jungle

Subjects: Hope/Obedience/Obstacles/Trust
Scripture Reference: Ps. 28: 7 & Isa. 41: 10

One morning, I envisioned myself standing on the edge of a vast and ferocious jungle. I knew immediately that the jungle represented life. As I stood there, knowing full well that I had to walk through it (through life), I could hear the sounds of the beasts in the jungle and could sense all of the dangers that lie ahead, e.g., quick sand and snares.

Jesus, who was standing beside me, explained that He had been through "there" and that He knew the way. He could take me safely across to the other side. If I wanted Him to carry me, I would have to wear a blindfold. If I did not wear the blindfold, I would see things that would frighten me so much, that I would jump off His back, start running and be devoured. He continued to explain that I would hear sounds that would frighten me. Nevertheless, I was to remain steadfast, keeping all my trust in Him. He said that He would not forsake me nor allow any harm to come to me as long as I remained on His shoulders and trusted Him. Then, in my heart, I heard Him say: "Would you like for me to carry you?"

How could I have refused such an offer? I could have tried it on my own but I knew I could never make it. One wrong move and I would be devoured! What an honor for Jesus to have extended such a blessed offer to me—one of the least of them! Be assured, I accepted His offer and have been riding on His shoulders ever since. During my life, I have heard many sounds that frightened me and I have been tempted to break and run. However, I know full well that my only real chance and my only real hope, is in Him.

Dear friend, His invitation was not only to me, it is extended to you. Jesus is your only real chance and your only real hope. Put on the blindfold and climb on His shoulders. Your life, though frightening, from time to time, will be a safe and a beautiful journey.

Precious last hours

Subjects: Circumstances/Death/Purpose/Suffering/
Understanding/Witnessing
Scripture Reference: Rom. 8: 28 & 2 Cor. 4: 17

While pastoring a small church in the mountains of West Virginia one of the laymen came to visit me. He was a very genuine Christian man who meant very much to me, the community and the church.

Tears welled up in his eyes as he looked to me for answers. His mother was in her late eighties. She was a Christian who had lived her entire life for the Lord. Now, as she was nearing the end of her life, one would believe that God would make her death a pleasant and easy one; however, this was not the case.

This fine old Christian lady had bone cancer. Her pain was unbearable and she had been suffering for well over a year. It appeared as though she was being punished by God—certainly not rewarded! This is what the layman came to talk to me about. He wanted to know why God would allow such a sweet, beautiful Christian lady to endure such pain. "Why doesn't God just take her home? She is ready. She deserves to be blessed, not punished!"

I honestly had no answer for him. In fact, I agreed! It did not make any sense to me either. God should reward her for her faithful life of service by taking her gently in the night. All I could tell my good friend was that God had His reasons. I also explained that God is far more concerned about spiritual matters than He is physical matters. I assured Him that God must have a spiritual reason for all of this.

About six months after our talk, his mother died in a hospital. Her pain grew so unbearable that when she was in the hospital, she had to have an orderly with her every moment, right by her side. The orderly that came on duty at 11:00 o'clock that night had a very bad reputation in the community. He was a known drug dealer and a thief! Some community members even went to the hospital administrator in an attempt to have him dismissed. A person with such a bad reputation should never be allowed to work in a hospital as an orderly. Their concern was that he would steal the drugs that were supposed to be administered to the patients.

All night long he sat with this lovely old lady. Her pain was so bad that she could not sleep so she just talked. She told him all about the Lord and how the Lord saved her and blessed her with a wonderful life and a wonderful family. About 5:30 in the morning she looked at the orderly and asked him if he would like to pray the prayer of salvation with her. He told her that he would like that very much so he knelt down beside her bed.

She laid her feeble hand on his head and led him in the sinner's prayer. When he said amen, her hand slipped off his head and she went to be with the Lord.

The orderly shared all of this at her funeral. My question to those who were in attendance was a simple one: "Do you think that she was happy to have endured the pain and suffering for this one soul?"

Today, that young man is the pastor of a church and has a tremendous ministry to the young people in his community who are known to be drug dealers and thieves.

If He orders, He pays

Subjects: Direction (Divine)/Goodness/
**   Misunderstanding/Obedience/Service/Works**
Scripture Reference: Mt. 7: 21-23 & 1 Thess. 5: 24

On several occasions, after observing the needs of the community, it became apparent that "helps" ministries needed to be provided for the hurting. For example, many people were hungry and malnourished so I set up a "food bank" program. Many were poor and had little or badly worn clothing, so I set up a "clothes closet." Both of these ministries failed, along with several others which, in order to meet a need, I started. We simply could not pay the bills.

No one was giving and I was very angry at God for not touching people's hearts and causing them to give. These were "good" ministries! While praying for God's help, He showed me something that left a feeling which can only be described as being doused with a bucket of ice water.

I saw a banker sitting at his desk and a man, apparently a building contractor, was seated in front of him. The banker reached behind his desk, pulled out a set of blueprints and handed them to the man. It was the plan for a branch bank which was to be built on the north side of town.

The banker told him where the building site was located and told the contractor to build it. When the building was completed, it was beautiful and would serve quite well as a branch bank. When the contractor presented the bill to the banker, he was paid, in full, right then and there. What could all this mean? What was the Lord trying to teach me? It was not clear to me so the Lord took me further.

The contractor drove past the new branch bank on several occasions. He was very impressed. Many people were visiting and business was "booming." Then, the contractor said: "This is good! This is meeting a tremendous need in the community!" It was so good, in fact, that he selected another site where he thought a branch was needed and built another building just like the first.

When he presented the banker with the bill, the banker was appalled and refused to pay, stating: "I did not order this and I am not paying for it." The contractor said: "But it's good and it will meet a real need." To this, the banker responded: "I know it is good and I know it will meet a need, but I did not order it and I am not paying for it!"

God is like the banker, if He orders something, He will provide the money for it. However, you must never expect Him to pay the bills for ministries and good deeds that you think are needed. He does not pay for good things, He pays for things He orders.

Awake up call

Subjects: Attitude/Circumstances/Confidence/
Encouragement/Purpose/Talents
Scripture Reference: Mt. 25: 14-30; Mk. 12: 42-44

While on a long trip in our family automobile, our children (ages 11 and 5) asked me to tell them a story. I could not think of one so I made one up. I could not pass up the opportunity to teach them one of God's principles. I chose the principle of using the talents that God has given us.

With Matthew 25:15 in mind, I told them the following story:

Once upon a time there was a very young rooster named Billy Clyde. He was proud to be a rooster but no one ever told him his main purpose. He just walked around the barnyard looking important. One day, the head rooster took Billy Clyde aside for a rooster-to-rooster talk. He explained that one of a rooster's main responsibilities is to wake the farmer up right at sunrise.

He told the young rooster that if he failed in his responsibility to wake up the farmer that the entire farm would collapse. In essence, the success of the farm laid primarily on the shoulders of the rooster.

Billy Clyde asked the head rooster "How do you wake him up?" He said: "I will come and get you early tomorrow morning and I will show you how to do it."

Early the next morning, before the sun arose, the head rooster and Billy Clyde made their way along the fence that circled the back side of the farmer's house. They watched together until they saw the first sign of the sun. Then, to the top of his lungs, the head rooster shouted: "Cock-a-doodle-do." He kept doing it and doing it until the farmer woke up.

All of this made Billy Clyde feel very special. He had a purpose and was a rooster with great responsibility. He decided that he better start practicing. However, every time he tried to shout: "Cock-a-doodle-do," all he could get out was: "Caw, Caw, Caw." He was embarrassed because he was the laughing stock of the whole barnyard.

Depressed, he went out into the woods and sat under a tree. A squirrel came to him and tried to teach him. In fact, the squirrel could shout: "Cock-a-doodle-do" perfectly–he sounded just like the head rooster! Not Billy Clyde! Just the same old: "Caw, Caw, Caw" time after time. A rabbit even tried to help. Like the squirrel, the rabbit could do it just fine.

Everyone was about to give up on Billy Clyde. He just could not cut it as a rooster–he could not do what he was created to do. Poor Billy Clyde had little to live for. He just wanted to die. Then, a wise old owl came and whispered something in his ear–something that changed his life.

Very, very early the next morning, Billy Clyde made his way to the very top of the barn. From there, he would be the first to see light from the rising sun. He watched intently! Finally, he saw it! The rising sun! He ran down the roof, dashed across the fence and flew across the barnyard to the back of the farmer's house. He threw open the window, jumped on the farmer's bed, pulled down the covers and yelled in the farmer's ear: "Caw, Caw, Caw!"

I explained to the boys that sometimes we do not always have everything we think we need in order to fulfill our responsibilities. However, God expects us to use the resources He has entrusted to us. Some, for example, cannot see, others cannot hear. Nevertheless, we all have a purpose and we all have a responsibility. We all have to accomplish the mission for which God has created us. No excuses, no cop outs, just do it—you will be glad you did!

Have no fear

**Subjects: Encouragement/Fact/Faith/Feelings/Hope/
          Protection (Divine)/ Responsibility**
Scripture Reference: Ps. 118: 1, 8

One morning during my meditations, when I was alone with the Lord, He showed me something that was very encouraging. I saw ten ladies in light military attire standing in formation at the bottom of a vast valley. The only weapons they had were swords that were in a sheath, fastened to a waist belt. They had no helmets or any other type of protective armor. Alongside them sat a man on a beautiful white horse. I thought He might be the Lord.

As I scanned the valley, I saw that they were totally encompassed by an army of men on horses who surrounded the ridge above them. These men were men of war. They had full body armor and weapons of every kind. It was apparent that they were about to attack the female soldiers, who did not have a chance. They were outnumbered three thousand to one. Their situation was perilous.

They looked at the man on the horse as if to say: "What are we to do?" Then, I heard Him say: "Have no fear, offer no resistance, they cannot harm you." As I continued to meditate, I could actually taste what it is to have faith. Have no fear? Offer no resistance? They cannot harm you! Who could just stand there while being attacked by such an army? Nevertheless, that is exactly what He told them to do. Then the charge began and it was an awful sight! In the midst of the dust, I could see swords and spears flying everywhere. It appeared to be a total massacre!

When the dust settled, however, all of the men in the attacking army lay dead. Nine of the young women were still standing, swords affixed to their waist (untouched) and none of them had a scratch! One of the young ladies had lost her faith and surrendered to the fear which had overwhelmed her. In an attempt at self-defense, she had drawn her sword and ran. While running, she had fallen and broke her neck, but received no wounds from the attacking soldiers. Her fear and lack of faith killed her.

It is hard to put our trust in the Lord when everything around us looks bleak and hopeless. However, if we place our faith and trust in Him, somehow, some way, He will see us through. The Lord is faithful and just.

An attitude adjustment

**Subjects: Attitude/Caring/Complaining/Humility/
Misunderstanding/Obedience/Pride/Service**
Scripture Reference: 2 Cor. 9: 7 & Eph. 6: 6

While I was pastoring a United Methodist Church in Eastern North Carolina, I tried to do everything I could to minister to the needs of my congregation. However, there seemed to be a pattern that continually emerged. That is, the members who gave the most needed and expected very little attention; however, those who gave the least were constantly in need of my time and attention.

One night, about one o'clock in the morning, my telephone rang. The caller was a lady whose name was on our membership roster but never attended church services. I had visited her on a couple of occasions and she made it quite clear that church attendance and involvement was not on her list of priorities. She was very well-known in the community and very wealthy. I am not sure if she ever contributed one dime to our church while I was pastor–at least up until this point.

She was crying and told me that she did not want to live anymore. It did not take me long to realize that this lady was dead serious. She really needed help and she needed it right then and there.

I got dressed and walked out of the house towards the car in a rain storm. As I was driving towards her home, the wiper blades were flapping back and forth and so was my attitude! To be perfectly honest, I was what the "old timers" call bellyaching.

"Boy! If this isn't something! I have to get up in the middle of the night, in the rain, to help someone who could not care less about me or the church. She is a self-centered, selfish, unthoughtful jerk! She was never there for the church but she sure expects the church to be there for her!" Over and over I kept complaining about being so used.

Then, I heard this still, small voice saying something like: "Why don't you go back and go to bed? Do you think I cannot find someone else to help her? Do you think I cannot orchestrate this universe without you?" At that point, I felt pretty small and realized that I was not doing too bad with selfishness myself. Did I want to be in the Lord's service or not? This was, indeed, a wake up call, not from the lady, it was coming from the Lord. It was not only raining outside, it was raining in my heart.

I pulled the car over on to the shoulder of the road and asked the Lord to forgive me. I asked Him if I could still go and minister to the lady, promising a better attitude. He let me know, in no uncertain terms, that He was more interested in my attitude of service than He was in my quantity of service. However, He told me I could still go if I would count it a joy and a privilege to be in His service.

From that moment on, I coined a new friendly phrase for myself in order to remain in check. "Dick, if you are going to do it, do it with a glad and dancing heart; otherwise, go home and go to bed."

A priceless gift

Subjects: Happiness/Joy/Knowledge/Misperception/
Reality/Salvation/Truth
Scripture Reference: Mt. 6: 21 & 2 Cor. 9: 15

One day, while in worship and in the presence of the Lord, He showed me a precious example which had a deep spiritual meaning.

I saw an elderly lady cleaning her house. Someone came to her door and presented her with a gift. It was a mantel-size grandfather clock. She accepted the gift graciously, thanked the giver and closed the door. She looked at the gift and found it to be very nice, so she re-arranged the other pieces on her mantel and set the clock right in the middle. There, it remained for all visitors to see.

She had many treasured possessions, which, in her estimation were far more valuable than the grandfather clock. In fact, when visitors would mention the grandfather clock she would say something like: "Yes, that is very nice, but look at this picture by Van Gogh." She even positioned the furniture around her more treasured possessions in order to call attention to them. They were very important to her and they were the things she wanted to talk about, not the grandfather clock.

Then, one day, while she was cleaning and dusting, she took the grandfather clock off the mantel and began to examine it more closely. To her utter amazement, she discovered it was hand engraved, inlaid with solid gold, and studded with diamonds, rubies and pearls–real ones!

Immediately, she realized that this gift, this grandfather clock, was the most valuable possession of all. It was far more valuable than her Van Gogh! She became very excited and re-arranged her entire house so that the clock became the focal point. No matter where you sat, you faced this treasured gift and now, it was all she wanted to talk about. Her Van Gogh and other previously considered treasures became unimpor-tant to her in the face of this new discovery.

The Lord showed me that the grandfather clock represented Him. There are many people who receive Him as Lord and Savior but He does not become the main focal point of their lives.

They are deceived, thinking there are other things in their lives that are more valuable than Jesus. Perhaps someday, they will examine the precious gift of salvation and discover it to be the most valuable treasure they could have. When this happens, they will re-arrange their lives so that He is all that others will be able to see when around them. He will be all that they will want to talk about–their "pearl of great price."

The shortest distance

Subjects: **Direction (Divine)/Guidance (Divine)/**
Obstacles/Understanding/Wisdom (Divine)
Scripture Reference: Ps. 119: 35 & Isa. 55: 8

The Lord showed me a house. I was standing out by the road and there was nothing (that I could see) between me and the front door except a well-kept lawn.

I have always been told that the shortest distance between two points is a straight line. However, individuals who are being divinely directed must dispose of that notion from time to time. God is looking down from above and sometimes He sees obstacles that are not in our view.

In this particular case, He showed me that the shortest distance was to follow the outer perimeter of the lawn, go all the way around the back and in the back door. He showed me that it would take me much longer to walk straight across the lawn and in the front door. Apparently, there was something in my path that I could not see.

The Lord helped me to understand that there would be times when His ways would not be my ways. He showed me that, in the future, when He instructs me to do something that did not make sense to me, that I would need to trust Him and to obey His orders–whether it made sense to me or not.

The Walls Came Down

**Subjects: Caring/Evangelism/Faith/Hope/Mercy/
         Salvation**
Scripture Reference: Josh. 6: 20 & Heb. 11: 30

While visiting a church on the eastern seaboard of North Carolina I had a very special experience. It happened during the worship service while the congregation was singing some very uplifting songs. I heard the Lord speak very clearly to my heart telling me that He was doing a new thing. He showed me that He wanted me to go and tell His people. I did not know what He meant and I just said: "Lord?" Then, this is what my heart heard: "As in the days of Jericho, when Joshua walked around that great city seven times and the walls came crashing down, I, too, will walk around your loved ones seven times and their walls will come crashing down."

My spirit was filled with understanding. Many of my loved ones had walls, barriers so strong that they were not even open to hear the Gospel. I knew in my spirit that these walls were created by two major problems. The first was bricks laid on bricks because of witnessing the actions of Christians. Professing Christians, for example, preaching one thing and doing another. When others see this, they set up barriers between themselves and God with statements like: "If that is Christianity, I want no part of it."

Secondly, walls are built between our loved ones and the Lord because of misunderstanding and pain. People naturally blame God for bad things. When they see a child starving to death, they say things like, "I will never serve a God who lets things like this happen." These two things cause very strong walls to be built. He showed me that He wants to tear the walls down and that He wants our help. Our involvement in the salvation of man is a part of His plan.

As this new understanding welled up within me, the Lord continued to speak to my heart. He showed me that I needed to pray for my loved ones. No, not just pray some simple two or three minute prayer. It was much more complex than that. He showed me that I needed to get on my face and pray for them until my burden for their soul was as great as His. He showed me that when my love and burden for them was as great as His, it would open the doors and He (Jesus) would personally go to my loved ones and physically walk around them seven times until their walls came tumbling down.

He touched my heart and showed me that this new promise was not just for me and my loved ones, but for anyone who would pray and seriously take on the burden for a lost loved one. Could this be true? Could God really be telling me this? How could I know this was really the Lord speaking to me and not just something that I was thinking up in my own mind. As I was pondering the validity of all that was happening, the worship leader stopped the service and said: "The Lord just spoke to my heart and told me that we need to join together and sing a very special song. The music started playing and the worship leader started singing "Jericho, Jericho, and the walls came tumbling down!" I thought I was going to take off and fly! Nothing like this had ever happened to me, but I knew it was the Lord.

I shared the experience with Pat Robertson, whom I worked for at the time, and he asked me to share it with all the employees at C.B.N., which I did at the next staff prayer meeting. There were about 900 people in the meeting and God's anointing on the entire incident was quite evident. One of the men who worked for C.B.N. was a Messianic Jew. He listened intently to the message. When he received Jesus as his Savior, his family renounced him. In fact, they had a funeral for him and considered him to be dead. Later in his life, his father died and he was not allowed to attend the funeral.

When his mother grew old, she was placed in a Jewish nursing home. It would have been virtually impossible for anyone to ever reach her with the Gospel of Jesus Christ. He was certainly not allowed anywhere near her.

After hearing the message, the young man went home and laid on his face before the Lord for seven or eight hours. He prayed and prayed for his dear mother's soul. His burden for her was so great that he cried until his body was exhausted.

The next day the most wonderful thing happened. He was sitting in his living room on Sunday afternoon and his telephone rang. He heard the voice of what sounded like a very old and weak woman. The voice said: "Son? Son, is that you?" He said: "Mama?" Then came the most beautiful words he had ever heard in his life: "Son, I just wanted to call and tell you that I just received Jesus as my personal Savior."

Sign over door

Subjects: Caring/Encouragement/Love/Thankfulness
Scripture Reference: Jer. 13: 20

When appointed as the pastor of a church (six during my 30 years of full-time ministry), the first thing I always did was to post a sign over the front doors of the church. It read:

> *"Through these doors pass the most*
> *beautiful people on earth, my*
> *congregation."   Rev. Arno*

I always thought that we should get started out on the right foot. I wanted them to know just what I thought of them.

Setting our sights too low

Subjects: Compromise/Favor (Divine)/Humility/
**   Priorities**
Scripture Reference: Mt. 7: 7

Pat Robertson, the President and Founder of the Christian Broadcasting Network in Virginia Beach, Virginia, was on his way to Atlanta to have dinner with me. At that time, I served as C.B.N.'s Spiritual Life Director for the states of Alabama and Georgia.

On the way to the airport, where I was to pick him up, I asked the Lord to give me favor with Pat Robertson. We had an excellent time together that evening and God's anointing seemed to be on everything we discussed regarding ministry plans.

When our time together concluded, I took him back to the airport and had an opportunity to pray for him and his family just before he boarded the plane.

I remember thinking on the way home just how much Pat Robertson seemed to like and respect me. Then I said, to the Lord: "Father, I asked you to give me favor with Pat Robertson and you did. Thank you." Then my heart and mind filled with the following words: "Yes, you asked me to give you favor with him and I did (pause) you could have had favor with me."

Needless to say, I have never prayed for favor with any man since then. I only seek God's favor and I ask Him to give it to me every morning of my life. He does.

Arise and go forth!

**Subjects: Direction (Divine)/Guidance (Divine)/
            Obedience**
Scripture Reference: Mt. 28: 19-20

One night, while I was praying, I was caught up in a spiritual experience which changed the direction of my life.

At the time, I was the Spiritual Life Director and the Administrator of the National Counseling Division for The 700 Club (Christian Broadcasting Network) in Virginia Beach, Virginia. It was an excellent position and I believed, at the time, that the Lord was using me and I was in utopia. However, it would soon be evident that He was entrusting me to an even more responsible position. As I prayed, I saw what appeared to me to be a flying stage coach. It was coming towards me at a high rate of speed with a driver sitting on the top of it just like you might see in an old western movie.

As the object passed by, I reached out and grabbed hold of a solid gold handrail and swung to the back of the coach. I found myself between two men who appeared to be elders. They were dressed in black and very stern looking. They did not speak or even acknowledge my presence. Their eyes were fixed straight ahead and their long black tuxedo looking jackets waved in the wind.

The very next moment, I found myself standing in some type of vestibule. It was a little room similar to where a pastor would wait prior to entering the sanctuary. Another man was present with me. He was very pleasant and accommodating. His job was to prepare me to enter into the sanctuary of God. He gave me a robe and began instructions. He explained that he would open the curtain and that I was to enter the room, turn to the left, walk to the center and then turn to the right. He told me that I was to walk towards God's throne and bow on bended knees.

As I approached the throne, I saw, over in the left corner, at least eight more elders–perhaps twelve. They were disgusted with the entire matter and were complaining about God's choice. I could hear them saying things like: "He is not capable and He will fail!"

The next event astonished me. I had been told clearly to bow on both knees. However, my left knee went to the floor and my right leg bent. I crossed my arms over my right knee and remained in this semi-respectful position. I was appalled at myself! I was in the presence of God and should have buried my face to the floor. What audacity to bend only one knee when in the presence of my Creator!

At that moment, the Lord God reached behind His throne and pulled out a beautiful gold sword. He placed the tip of it on my right shoulder and then on my left. With that, He said: "I commission you a Commander. Arise and go forth." He then handed me a scroll which was secured with a red ribbon. Immediately, I found myself standing on terrain which appeared to me to be Israel. I really thought I was in Israel and shouted out loud: "It's Israel!" Then, just as suddenly, I found myself back in the throne room. One of the elders came towards me, grabbed the scroll from my hands and said: "I knew he could not do it!"

The Lord God reached over and took the scroll from the elder, removed the red ribbon and replaced it with a green ribbon and handed it back to me again. Then He said: "I will give you everything you need, go forth on July 12th."

The year was 1981. I resigned my position at C.B.N. and on July 12th, I began the foundation work for the National Christian Counselors Association. I believe that this is my Israel and that: "EQUIPPING CHRISTIANS TO COUNSEL THE HURTING" is my life's mission.

On July 12, 1992, eleven years later, my wife, Phyllis, and I, founded the Sarasota Academy of Christian Counseling. The S.A.C.C. expands the outreach and training opportunities of our world-wide ministry.

The garden variety

Subjects: **Forgiveness/Happiness/Peace/Restoration/**
Victory
Scripture Reference: Mt. 18: 18

One of the greatest challenges I faced during my ministry was encouraging people to forgive others. They always seemed to have an excellent excuse to be angry and resentful. Over and over, I would watch their happiness drift away in an exchange for bitterness.

I asked the Lord to show me the secrets about forgiveness–to reveal the mystery. My heart and mind was flooded with a new understanding. Forgiveness, He showed me, is a gift to the person who was hurt or betrayed. Most people see it as a gift to the perpetrator but it is not. It is a gift to the victim. God created forgiveness as a way of restoring someone's happiness after it was torn asunder by the sin of another.

The Lord showed me a beautiful garden in which a man planted corn, tomatoes, peas and other nourishing vegetables. During the night, another man came and sowed weeds in the beautiful garden. The weeds came up quickly and were stealing the nutrition needed by the vegetables and they were beginning to die out.

God gave the man a choice. He could sit and grumble and complain about how unfairly he was treated. He certainly had the right to do so and no one would blame him. Or, he could do something about it. He worked very hard to plant and cultivate the garden and it was all for nothing unless he took positive action.

At first, he took a pair of shears and cut the tops off all the weeds. This, of course, did not help. The roots were still alive and still stealing nutrition from the vegetables. Then he pulled the weeds up by the roots and threw them outside of the garden area. With this, his vegetables began to thrive and he reaped a wonderful harvest. He was not doing a favor for the person who tried to destroy the garden, he was doing a favor for himself and he reaped the benefits. If he would have held on to his rights to sit and complain and do nothing, his garden would have been lost.

I began to understand that the Lord was imparting a beautiful teaching to me. The vegetable garden represented a person's "garden" of happiness. They try so hard to be happy and then someone comes along and sows something that can destroy it. If we simply forgive them, it is like cutting the top off a weed. We need to forgive the person AND to ask the Lord to forgive them for trespassing against us. This is commonly referred to as tri-lateral forgiveness.

In Matthew 18:18, Jesus said: "Verily I say unto you, Whatsoever ye shall bind on earth shall be bound in Heaven: and whatsoever ye shall loose on earth shall be loosed in Heaven."

Just saying something like "I forgive Joe for what he did" is not exercising our authority to "loose" them. This only happens when we ask God to "loose" them (forgive them) for what they have done to us. Throughout my ministry I have heard people say: "I will forgive them, but I cannot forget it."

When the man with the vegetable garden pulled the weeds up by the roots, he threw them outside of his garden area but they were still on his property. They laid there until the sun dried them up. When we forgive someone and ask God to forgive them and to release them from all accountability for what they did to us, the trespass has been pulled up by the roots–eternally erased, as though it never happened. It remains in our being (memory) for a time, but eventually, the "Son" dries the memory up. If it is erased from history, then the memory of it fades with time.

Once we have exercised our authority and time passes, we often have a difficult time recalling the name of the person who sinned against us. We are set free and do not have to relinquish our happiness. Because of the gift of forgiveness, we are restored just like the Scripture says: "He restoreth my soul." To my surprise, the Lord added one other thing. He told me that we plant weeds in our own "garden" of happiness by committing sin. It is not enough to ask God to forgive us–this is only half of the forgiveness process. We have to "tri-laterally" forgive ourselves.

The dark room

Subjects: Forgiveness/Happiness/Peace/Repentance/ Restoration
Scripture Reference: Ezek. 18: 31a

While meditating one day and seeking the help of the Holy Spirit for my Sunday morning message, I received a beautiful word from the Lord regarding repentance.

He showed me a woman who was locked up in a dark room. The room had no windows and only one door. The dark room represented a place of unhappiness and despair and she was put in there by someone else. Someone had committed a sin against her and here she stayed. At one point in her life she lived on the outside of this room, in the sunshine and fresh air (representing a time of joy and happiness).

God did not want her to be locked up in this dark room. He wanted her to be free and happy just as she once was. The Lord provided two things for this woman: light so she could find the door and a key so she could unlock it and escape. The light was forgiveness and the key was repentance. Someone else committed a sin against her, however, she also committed a sin for the way she responded to their action.

She could not be totally free until she repented for her sinful response.

Getting started

Subjects: Devotions/Tithing
Scripture Reference: Jas. 5: 11

One day I was talking to a man who made his living as a coal miner. He told me that he spent most of his life underground, down in the mines. He was somewhat older now and the coal company provided him with a new job. He ran the conveyer belt that moved the coal from the mouth of the mine to the trucks or to the storage heaps.

One of the things he told me was quite enlightening. He explained that if he shut the belts down at night when they were fully loaded with coal, it would take a lot of momentum to start them the next day. In fact, he explained that he had five engines to run the belt. He had to use all five of them just to start a fully loaded conveyer belt to move. Once the belt was moving, he could shut four of them off and keep it going, fully loaded, all day long with just one engine.

This applies to so many areas of life! It takes a great deal to start something in motion–especially something good and something that will bring glory to our heavenly Father. However, once it is in motion, it takes very little to keep it going.

Two of the most difficult things that a Christian can start doing is having devotions and tithing. Once, however, these practices are set in motion, they are the sweetest and easiest things a person can do. Momentum! Ask the Lord for the additional strength you need and He will help you GET IT STARTED.

Great works won't help

Subjects: Death/Eternal life/Salvation/Works
Scripture Reference: Eph. 2: 8-9

I attended the funeral of a minister who dedicated his entire life to the Lord's service. He was a precious brother and lived to be a very old man. He was ministering to others the day he died.

After the funeral, several men gathered together out in front of the church. One of the men said: "Well, do you think old Charlie made it?" One of the other men said: "If he did, it wasn't because of his beautiful white hair and it wasn't because he served the Lord all of his life. It was because of Jesus. It was because he repented of his sins and received Jesus as his Savior. Nothing else could have saved him—nothing but the blood of Jesus."

A helping hand

Subjects: Circumstances/Confidence/Contentment/
Protection (Divine)/Security
Scripture Reference: Ps. 91: 4

One morning, I read Psalms 46: 1-5 and the Lord gave me a vision. I saw myself standing with my feet planted on the earth. I had my right arm stretched towards Heaven and Jesus had my hand in His.

Suddenly, the world was removed from beneath my feet. However, I did not move and was not shaken. My feet were not fixed to the earth (things of the world), they were fixed to that which is far above the earth—eternal.

Those who are fixed to the things of the world will fall when it falls. They will be tossed with every ebb and flow of the tide, from the fluctuation of the stock market to the unstable weather patterns. However, those whose trust is in the Lord will stand and not be moved.

Wild things

Subjects: Circumstances/Control/Foolishness
Scripture Reference: Acts 9: 5

The Lord showed me a young lady who owned a beautiful stallion. While riding it one day, it began to bolt and she was thrown backwards.

She managed to grab firmly to the stallion's tail and was being dragged behind it as it raced across the fields. When I saw what was happening, I started screaming: "Let go, let go, he is going to kill you!" She shouted back: "No, I'm not going to let go! He's mine!"

Sometimes we hold on to things that are destroying us just because we think they "belong to us" or because we feel we have the "right" to hold on to them. Jesus told Paul in Acts 9:5: "it is hard for thee to kick against the pricks."

 We need to let go and let God. In His time and in His way, He will work it all out for our good."

A wild stallion

Subjects: Discipline/Obedience/Righteousness/Sin
Scripture Reference: Lk. 9: 62 & Heb. 10: 38

Very few things are more beautiful than to see a wild stallion out on a range. He will move with a sense of freedom and such grace that it is almost breath-taking.

The same beautiful stallion, however, when moving through a flower garden, is not so beautiful. He destroys everything in his path. His grace turns into destruction and his beauty becomes repulsive.

Christians are beautiful! There is, however, nothing in the world quite as ugly as a Christian who is living in sin.

The bridge is out!

Subjects: Control/Fact/Hell/Misperception/
Protection (Divine)/Understanding
Scripture Reference: Ezek. 33: 9

A lot of people truly resent the Gospel and they resent God. They feel that, if there is a God, He has placed desires within them and then will damn them eternally if they meet these desires.

I have always struggled with the fact that God created Hell for those who do not obey Him and live as He commands.

One day, He showed me a vision of a man who was standing on a curve of a highway. The man was waving a flag and shouting as cars passed by: "Stop! The bridge is out!" The man did not destroy the bridge that once lay just ahead. He was simply trying to save lives because he knew the bridge was out.

As some of the cars passed him by, the people shouted at him: "Don't you try to control my life." Or, "Liar!" They refused to listen and drove directly into the canyon wall.

Hell was never God's intention. Man's sin destroyed the bridge. God has appointed tens of thousands of "flagmen" (normally referred to as preachers) to warn all who will listen that danger lies ahead. Turn Around! This has been the message throughout the ages. It is a message sent by God because He loves us and His only desire is to save our souls from certain peril.

Carrying our yesterdays

Topics: Counseling/Limitations/Unforgiveness
Scripture Reference: Mt. 6: 34 & I Pet. 5: 7

Some of my Christian service was spent pastoring churches, however, most of it was in the area of counseling—some in private practice and some of it as a writer of textbooks teaching counseling methodologies.

I am constantly asked: "What is the difference between secular and Christian counseling?" Actually, the answer is quite simple. Secular counselors do not engage in Christian principles such as the principle of forgiveness. That is to say, secular counselors do not tell their counselees that they need to forgive. They instruct their counselees in what they consider "reality." For example, if you were raped by someone, then that is a reality from which you cannot escape. So what do you do? You learn to live with it, to carry it! Secular counseling is merely the practice of encouraging people to live with their past negative experiences—to carry them on their shoulders! After all, a person cannot lay them aside, because they actually happened.

Christian counseling, on the other hand, instructs the opposite. We understand that we cannot carry our yesterdays. Mankind was never created with the emotional ability to carry past experiences any more than we were created with the strength/ ability to lift a car. Remembering bad things is one thing, but living with the consequences and effects (carrying them on our shoulders) is another matter.

The Lord gave us something called forgiveness, a way out, a way to cast our cares at His feet and walk away clean. Forgiveness, contrary to what most people believe, is not a gift to the perpetrator, it is a gift from God to the victim—a gift which will set the victim free from all of the emotional and psychological devastation that the secular counselors say they must carry. Now the victims are free to regain what was stolen from them, their happiness.

Can you carry all of that bad stuff on your shoulders—not just the bad stuff that others did to you, but the bad stuff you did? You do not have to! You have a beautiful gift from God, it is called forgiveness.

Beautiful renewal

Topics: Hope/Renewal/Resurrection
Scripture Reference: Song 2: 12 & Jn. 2: 19

At the writing of this book, we are being told of devastating wild fires that are raging in many states—especially California where more than 1.5 million acres have already burned. It is difficult for us to comprehend 1.5 million acres. We live in Sarasota, Florida and this entire city covers less than 10,000 acres, and sometimes it takes nearly an hour to drive from one side to the other.

One would think that nothing good could ever come from such devastation. However, our Lord, in His infinite wisdom, planned ahead. You see, there are flower bulbs called ephemerals (Greek word meaning fleeting—lasting a very short time—a day) that will not come forth unless they are subjected to major heat such as that caused by wildfires. After the fire goes out, these magnificent, beautiful flowers of many species spring forth everywhere. They do not last very long, but they declare total renewal as if shouting "Be at peace, all is well." Then, the minerals restored to the soil begin to cause a miraculous rebirth upon the scorched and devastated earth. Our hope is restored.

This is precisely what happened on Calvary; out of the horror of Christ's torture, humiliation, and crucifixion, arose the utter beauty of salvation. This beauty however, is not ephemeral, it is everlasting.

Beyond comprehension!

Topics: Crucifixion/Pain/Suffering
Scripture Reference: Heb. 2: 9

Our oldest son, Rick, called me one day and shared something that changed his life. He told me that he was sanding a piece of wood and that he accidentally rammed a large splinter underneath one of his fingernails. He said: "Dad, the pain was so excruciating that it nearly knocked me unconscious, I honestly saw stars!" Then, with a noticeable tear in his voice, he said: "Oh God! What it must have been for Jesus on Calvary's cross! I cannot even comprehend!" After a short period of silence, he said the most beautiful words I ever heard him say: "Dad, He did it all for me!"

Lovin' grandma

Topics: Children/Love/Praise/Worship
Scripture Reference: Deut. 6: 5 & Lk. 18: 17

One day when my wife, Phyllis, and I were on a shopping excursion with our youngest grandson, Noah, who was safely strapped into his car seat, I was privileged to hear some wonderful words "out of the mouth of babes."

I dropped Phyllis off close to the door of the mall with the intentions of taking Noah with me as I parked the car. When she exited the vehicle, Noah, who was not quite three years old at the time, said: "Granddad! Don't hit her! I love her! (he dropped his little head down until his chin touched his chest and quietly continued) I love her so much!"

We need to become like little children too. We need to adore our Lord like this. From the very depths of our soul we need to bow our heads and confess: I Love Him! I Love Him So Much! Indeed, He is worthy of our adoration and praise.

He leadeth me

Topics: Control/Direction (Divine)/Guidance(Divine)/ Will (God's)/Will (Self)
Scripture Reference: Ps. 139: 13

> *"For thou hast possessed my reins:*
> *thou hast covered me in my mother's womb."* ...

I never feel more secure than I do when I read this scripture, imagine, He possesses our reins! He directs every step we take ("The steps of a good man are ordered by the Lord..." Ps 37: 23a). He leads us "beside the still waters." Of course, He will only hold your reins if you ask and surrender your life to Him. He will never interfere with your free will—you are even free to drive your life right into the ground, if that is your will.

A ship in shallow waters

Topics: Anchors/Burdens/Forgiveness/Happiness
Scripture Reference: Phil. 3:13

Sometimes we are like a ship in shallow waters, held there by our anchors. Our anchors normally consist of bad experiences that we have suffered. Some people (ships), for example, remain in very shallow, murky, stagnant waters because of the death of a loved one that they cannot overcome; the loss of employment; divorce; foreclosure of home, etc. However, if we are willing to forgive (perhaps even God) and lay these things at the feet of Jesus, the anchors will be cut away and our ship (life) can be free to sail into deep, healthy waters.

Remember, if you are holding onto something, then that "something" is also holding on to you. If you want to be set free, then let it go.

A memorable lesson

Topics: Children/Correction/Guidance (Children)/
**   Lessons**
Scripture Reference: Prov. 22: 6

Our youngest son, Jaysen, is a molecular geneticist, however; without some proper guidance, he could have been an arsonist!

He spent a couple of weeks with his Grandma Arno in Ohio one summer. During his stay, he found some blue tip matches in her kitchen and grabbed a pocketful of them. He was throwing them on concrete and against bricks on the side of the house and when they hit properly, they would ignite. He had a blast! Then, the unthinkable—Grandma caught him!

In her infinite and Godly wisdom, she went to the kitchen and retrieved a wooden cutting board—one that would serve as a perfect paddle. She held out her hand and told Jaysen to crack her with the makeshift paddle. He did not want to, but she insisted and, in fact, made him paddle her hand with intensity. When he asked her why, she said: "Because I need to be punished for not having taught you to never play with matches."

He now testifies that this experience was the most memorable (stinging) paddling he "never" had. It literally changed his life and set him on a course of excellence. What a Godly action! My son told me that he realized years later that her action was a metaphor for what Christ has done for us. He endured the punishment for the wrongs that we have done.

I had a wonderful mom—well, actually, because of Jesus, I still do. She's a wonderful grandma too! I know that God must love having her so close to Him.

A vision of hell

**Topics: Calvary/Damnation/Eternity/Heaven/Hell/
Paradise/Repentance/Salvation
Scripture Reference: Lk. 23: 32-33 & 39-43**

Most historical scholars agree that, according to the records which are available to us, there were two thieves crucified with Jesus. The thief on His right was named Demos and the one on His left was named Gestus.

I visited Calvary (Golgotha) one day in 1974 and it had, to say the least, a memorable impact on me. However, the Lord gave me a vision of Calvary on one occasion that made an even greater impact on my life than being there in person.

I saw three crosses up on the hill. The center cross and the one on the left (Christ's right), was empty, but the other one, the one on Christ's left, the one where Gestus was, had a man nailed to it—a man who was in excruciating pain! I couldn't believe my eyes! I protested to God! I said: "God! Jesus is on the wrong cross! He is supposed to be in the center!"

What followed left me speechless! It wasn't Jesus at all. In fact, what I was seeing was a present day picture. It was Gestus! Remember, he is the one who joined the crowd and mocked Jesus. The other one, Demos, asked Jesus to remember him when he came into His kingdom. To that Jesus replied: "Verily, I say unto thee, today shalt thou be with me in paradise."

Gestus joined the crowd and mocked Christ, and then everyone left him there! Jesus and Demos left for paradise, the Roman soldiers left to carry on their duties, and the crowd went on their merry way. Everyone was gone and there he was, all alone for all eternity—alone with nothing but his anguish. He was still bearing his cross, eternally in Hell!

Visiting the iniquity...

Topics: Anchors/Burdens/Heritage/Hope/Sin/
        Strongholds
Scripture Reference: Mt. 3: 10a & Ex. 20: 5-6

Many of our problems are a direct result of our past sins or the sins of our forefathers. These sins are commonly referred to as strongholds. You may, for example, suffer from emotional and/or physical problems because someone in your family (Dad, Mom, Grandfather, etc.) abused drugs. Regardless of the cause or the effect, it can stop with you, right now! It does not have to be passed on to your children. You can lay an axe to the root of your family tree and be set free from those strongholds. Jesus is the axe!

A bad massage

Topics: Education/Influence/Values
Scripture Reference: Mt. 22: 21 & 2 Cor. 6:14

I believe that persons, who want careers such as architect, engineer, medical doctor, etc., should attend colleges and universities that provide excellent academics and opportunities for those professions. However, persons who want to enter into full-time Christian service should not attend secular schools that teach humanism. If a person wants to serve the Lord, they should be taught by the Lord's servants.

I wrestled with this while I was attending Old Dominion University in Norfolk, Virginia. I was working on my Masters degree in Counseling and Guidance and learning secular techniques that were in direct opposition to the teachings of Jesus Christ. What was I doing there? I wanted to be a Christian counselor and to use the Bible as my foundation, not Sigmund Freud.

I went before the Lord in prayer and expressed my frustrations. What He laid on my heart was astonishing. He asked me if my heart and mind belonged to Him. I said: "Of course Lord, you know that they do." Then my heart was filled with words that cut to the core of my soul: "Then why are you laying yourself at the feet of the ungodly and allowing your heart and mind to be massaged by non-believers?"

How can non-believers teach us anything about values, human behavior or the purpose of life? How can non-believers teach us how to resolve our problems? They are humanists and they teach humanistic ways—ways that are contrary to our Holy Scriptures. Prayerfully, I will never allow a non-believer to massage my heart or mind again. Their ways are not God's ways, and therefore, not our ways.

His yoke is easy!

Topics: Guidance (Divine)/Will (God's)/Will (Self)
Scripture Reference: Mt. 11: 30

What did Jesus mean when He said that His yoke was easy? Jesus' earthly father, Joseph, was a carpenter and Jesus probably spent most of His time as a young man learning that same trade. And, when we picture Joseph as a carpenter we normally picture him as someone who crafted tables, chairs and other wooden objects. However, that was not the primary function of a carpenter in that day. Few persons know it, but carpenters were highly skilled at a much-needed craft.

Back in that day, the most valuable possession a person could have was an ox. If you owned an ox you were successful and considered wealthy. Each individual ox had to be form-fitted with a yoke. You could not just take a yoke off of one ox and put it on another. Their collarbones are very sensitive and can be easily damaged if the yoke does not fit precisely. Once an ox is damaged by an ill-fitting yoke, it is rendered worthless. That must never happen!

The carpenter was the person in the community who was responsible for properly measuring and molding the yoke so it would be "easy."

The Lord created us with a specific temperament—a temperament which would give us the natural abilities (Inclusion, which is social, Control, which is decision making and Affection, which is our ability to enter into deeper relationships) to fulfill His specific call on our individual lives. Because of our temperament, we can conclude that, while the work may be difficult, the yoke God created for us fits perfectly and is, simply put, "easy."

A bad reputation

Topics: Christ's Return/Eating/Second Coming/ Working
Scripture Reference: 2 Thess. 3: 10-11

Paul reminded the early Christians to be responsible individuals, to work and to earn their way. This was a desperate message for the time because most Christians were being seen as beggars. In fact, for a short time, the word Christian meant beggar! You see, they believed in the "perusia." What is the perusia? This is a Latin word which means the immediate (literally now, today, any second), return of Christ. Christians were not going to be caught out in the field working or caught off guard! No! They were literally looking skywards and they were convinced that Jesus would return any second, most certainly before lunch. When lunch time came, they had nothing to eat because they were not working. Then, they repeated this behavior throughout the afternoon—they did not work, they spent the afternoon looking for Jesus to come forth from the clouds, just as He had promised. That night, they had to beg for food. They were doing this day after day.

We must be faithful and be ready "for the hour cometh," however, we have responsibilities and the best way to honor Jesus is to be found working, not wanting and not gazing skyward. Christian are not beggars, they are dependable and responsible persons. The early church misunderstood the promise of the second coming and believed that to prove one's faithfulness, he or she must be watching and waiting for the perusia.

Denying Christ

Topics: Denial/Praying/Shame
Scripture Reference: Mt. 10: 33 & Mk. 8: 38

Sometimes we make quick decisions that we really regret later. On one occasion, our youngest son, Jaysen, was sitting in his biology class, waiting for the professor to hand out a mid-term exam. He had his head bowed as he prayed for the Lord to give him a clear mind and the ability to recall all the information he had learned. In other words, he was asking the Lord to help him pass the exam.

As the professor placed the written exam down on Jaysen's desk, he said: "Oh Jaysen, I am sorry to disturb you, were you praying?" Instantly and with little thought, Jaysen looked up at him and said: "No! I wasn't praying. I have a headache." Ugh! Denial!

Well, needless to say, the Holy Spirit wasn't very pleased! The conviction began! No sleep and no peace—not until this matter is resolved! So, back to campus he goes—right straight to the professor's office with his ego in tow. "Sir, may I have a moment? You see sir, I need to tell you something—I was praying to Jesus. I didn't get the headache until I lied to you about it."

"Oh", said the professor, "I am so glad you clarified that for me. You see, I am a Christian too. I am thrilled to learn that we share the same faith."

God's finger print

**Topics: Creation/Disposition/Genetics/Personality/
    Temperament
Scripture Reference: Ps. 139: 15-16**

One of Sigmund Freud's best known teachings is called Tabula Rasa. He theorized that we are all born a blank slate and that our character and personality are 100% "learned." That is to say that, we are merely a product of our environment.

Of course, the most respected universities in America have conducted studies that have proven that his theory was wrong. Nevertheless, most psychological approaches, theories, and techniques, still presume Freud's theory to be "sacred writings."

We are, in fact, born with a pre-disposition to the world around us and the Bible states this quite clearly. Some of us view our world, and the people who live in it, as threatening and non-trustworthy. Others hold with a totally opposite view and, from birth, are trusting and non-threatened. This pre-disposition to our environment is known as temperament. It can be seen in every aspect of our lives. Some people, by their very nature, are motivated by the promises of reward while others are motivated by the threat of punishment; still others by neither and still others by both. These unique differences can only be attributed to our Creator. They are not physical genetics; they are spiritual genetics and they clearly reveal the fingerprint of God on each and every individual on this planet.

Music to my ears

Topics: Beauty/Creation/Good (God)/Pleasure
Scripture Reference: Ps. 33: 5, 34: 8 & Jn. 10: 10

One morning I was singing in the shower. I have always believed that if we start out our day singing and praising God, that the day is always nicer. My wife and I also have devotions every morning and her favorite saying is: "If you do not start your day hemmed in with prayer, it will come unraveled." Beautiful!

On this particular morning, I was singing one of my favorite songs, God Is So Good. Suddenly, it hit me like a brick! God is good! My mind began dancing with thoughts of God's goodness. For example, I realized that the world we live in is gorgeous. We commonly have beautiful blue skies with cloud formations that take your breath away. We have flowers that are so stunning that we are moved by their elegance; rainbows; sunsets, and fruit trees; lovely green grass, and oceans lined with stunning blue-green hues that are simply magnificent.

Do we even understand that God could have created mankind and just placed us on a totally brown or dingy grey planet? Our planet could be little more than a rock. He made it so beautiful and gave us such a magnificent creation to live in because He loves us and wanted us to have, not only life, but life abundantly! The beautiful creation that we live in is a gift to man from God, just to make our lives more pleasurable. All that and a Saviour too!

God is so good! You know, He could be a mean god. We sing an old hymn and declare: "God in three persons, blessed Trinity." Listen to that again. God is a person, just like you and I are persons. He is a person and He is a good person.

Stretching a dollar

Topics: Giving/Law (God's)/Money/Tithing
Scripture Reference: Lev. 27: 30 & Mal. 3: 8-10

Most Christian theologians believe that Christians have been ordered by God to tithe and that we are still commanded to do so (even under the New Testament). Sadly, few Christians do tithe. Actually, I have never viewed tithing as a duty, but more of an honor.

The fact is that you cannot out-give God. As stated previously, I think it is wrong to tithe (or make offerings) with the hope of gain. However, it is a law that remains steadfast—you cannot out-give God.

I like to tithe because it gives me an opportunity to turn regular, secular money into holy money. If you work and earn $1.00 you can buy $1.00 worth of stuff. If, however, you tithe that $1.00 you will have $.90 of holy money. That $.90 will, by some miracle of God, have a purchasing power of something like $5.00. Your automobile tires will last longer, you will not have quite as many unexpected expenses, your milk does not spoil as fast—well, you get the idea. Honestly, I would much rather have a few pennies of holy money (residue of one's tithe) than a pocket full of unholy (un-tithed) money.

Setting up for a fall

**Topics: Disappointment/Expectations (Ungodly &
         Unrealistic)**
Scripture Reference: 1 Cor. 2: 9 & Ps. 62: 5

I had a precious mother and she was a God-fearing woman. She, however, had a noticeable Melancholy temperament. She always seemed let-down or disappointed. If we went out to dinner, it seemed like her meal was not quite what she had hoped for or expected. No matter what kind of car she had, she always "thought it would be a little shinier," or "have more cup holders."

Honestly, my dear mother always set herself up to be disappointed. Her expectations were unrealistic. I call it ungodly expectations and I always try to avoid it.

About a year after my mother died, my dad called me to say that he saw her standing in the living room. Of course, it was not my mother because that is unscriptural. At best, it could have been an angel whom God sent to bring my dad a sense of hope and peace, but it most certainly was not my mother standing there. Nevertheless, I asked dad what she looked like and he said: "That's the thing Dick! She did not look radiant to me. I even told her that she didn't." Dad went on to explain that when he asked her if she was happy in Heaven, she said: "it's not quite what I had hoped for."

Wow! The first words out of my mouth were: "I rebuke that in the name of Jesus Christ! Dad, that was not mom and it was not an angel sent from God. The Scriptures work in harmony to assure us that we cannot, with all our might, imagine how wonderful Heaven is going to be and, Dad, my mother could not have out-imagined God! There is no way in the world that she could have imagined anything greater than Heaven and then been disappointed."

My friend, ungodly expectations may plague people here on earth, but they will never exist in Heaven. Know this; you will never be disappointed in Heaven. It will be far greater than anything you can hope for or imagine.

While you are running

Topics: Grace/Grief/Tidings (Good)
Scripture Reference: 2 Sam. 18:19-21 & 32

Absalom was dead and someone had to tell the king of his
treasonous son's death.   The first runner that came forth,
Ahimaaz could run fast; however, he lacked finesse. Surely if
he took the king such bad tidings, he would stumble over the
announcement and the king would have him killed. No, the
general needed a runner who had grace—a runner who could
bare the tidings to the king properly and with gentleness. The
general called for Cushi!

But no, Ahimaaz was raring to run and he kept pestering the
general with requests to run. Seemingly, in disgust and without
thought, the general just told him to go. He was so fast that he
quickly overtook Cushi and was swiftly in the presence of King
David. He gave the king a complete account of the battle,
but the king was anxious for news of his son and he asked: "Is
the young man Absalom safe?" The response was vague and
the king became angry. Just then, Cushi arrived and reported
to the king with grace and excellence. When asked the awful
question regarding Absalom, he said this: "The enemies of my
lord the king, and all that rise against thee to do thee hurt, be
as that young man is."

His report provided the king with the information he had to
have—his son was dead. However, the report was executed
with such excellence that it also served to remind the king who
he was—the king; no one, not even the king's own son dare

war against him. The king's dignity was protected by the young runner.

We have a wonderful message to deliver too—a message of eternal hope. Christ has risen and through Him, we can have everlasting life. We must run with this message and we must run swiftly, but more importantly, we must deliver it with excellence and dignity–in a way that will honor our Lord, the King. We must remember while we are running, why we're running.

Victory over Satan

Topics: Demons/Possession/Satan
Scripture Reference: Mt. 12: 43-45a

During my 42 years of full-time Christian service, I have only had two absolute undeniable confrontations with a demon wherein I can honestly testify that I know with all certainty that I was in the presence of a demon.

We had a group of teenagers in our church called The Agape Share Group. As senior pastor, I formed the group and served as its director. There were about 30 teenagers in the group and we traveled in a church bus to nursing homes to sing and encourage the residents. We also sang at revivals and ministered at local events.

One Christmas, I gave each one of the members of the group a Christmas present. It was a large, gold clergy cross on a black string necklace. The cross measured three and a half inches in height—it was huge! However, they would go beautifully with their uniforms. As each member entered the church that night,

I met them at the front door, placed the cross around their necks, and greeted them with a hearty: "Merry Christmas!"

One of the leaders of the group, Diane, was an exceptional young Christian lady and what happened that night was indescribably shocking. After a few announcements, I asked everyone to join hands for prayer. Just as we bowed our heads, I heard the most demonic voice imaginable come out of Diane saying: "Take this off me—take this off me now!" When I looked at her, she was tugging at the string that held her new cross.

Immediately, I had her kneel at the altar and asked all of the other teenagers to join me in prayer for Diane. I had no idea how she could be possessed as none of this was theologically comprehensible. God and Satan could not possibility occupy the same soul. Nevertheless, I had a young lady at the altar of my church who was in serious trouble. This was not a time for theological debate; it was a time for action.

Seven times I commanded the demon to leave in the name of Jesus Christ, and seven times there was a sense of peace and tranquility followed by that horrible, chilling voice saying: "Take this off me, take this off me now!"

How could this be? How could this demon remain in her? Then I realized that he was the eighth demon and the captain of some kind of a squad of satanic servants that had overtaken this young girl. The other seven demons left on command, however, this demon, was strong and obstinate. I turned and faced the cross that graced our sanctuary and I said: "Jesus! I need you to personally come and take authority over this demon, he is too strong for me!" Just then, I was filled with the Holy Ghost and I spun around on the heels of my shoes, laid my hand on her head, and with the total authority of Jesus

Christ Himself, said: "Out! Now!" Just then, the front door of the church opened up and then slammed shut as though it was coming off its hinges. I ran and opened the door and looked all around the church in every direction but there was no one there. I believe with all of my heart that Jesus showed me, Diane, and all of the teenagers present that night that all the demons were gone, even their captain.

I am happy to report that, to this very day, Diane is a lovely Christian person who serves Jesus faithfully and honorably.

Having a lofty title

Topics: Ego/Offices/Pride/Titles
Scripture Reference: Mt. 23: 11 & Jude 1: 1a

Most theologians agree that Jude was, in fact, the younger earthly brother of Jesus. However, instead of laying claim to that office—being his brother, Jude introduces himself as: "(I) Jude, the servant of Jesus Christ, and brother of James, ..."

This is a lesson from which we could all gain. We want to be called reverend, pastor, doctor, attorney, senator, or, perhaps, president, but Jude had no need for those kind of titles. No, Jude recognized that there was a title (office) higher than all of these, even higher than being the earthly brother of Jesus Christ, the title of servant. We would all do well to lay claim to this office and understand that it is, in fact, the highest office we can hold. Remember, Jesus said: "But he that is greatest among you shall be your servant."

Enjoying retirement

Topics: Death/Preaching/Rest/Retirement/Works
Scripture Reference: Jn. 9: 4 & Phil. 3: 14

I had visions of retiring when I turned 65 years of age, but so far my grade for that is "F." My wife tells people that: "He is only working half days now—twelve hours!" That seems to be true. One wise old preacher asked: "How do Christians know when their work on earth is done? They are dead!" We need to keep pressing on toward the high mark as long as we have breath. We are so blessed to be saved and we need to share the good news with everyone we meet and to declare Jesus with every breath we take.

Dr. Richard G. Arno

PART FOUR

EVANGELISM

Scripture Reference: Eccl. 3:11 & Mt. 28: 19-20

The standard dictionary definition of EVANGELISM is "the zealous preaching or spreading of the Gospel."

The standard dictionary definition of EVANGELIZE is "to convert to Christianity."

To evangelize is to boldly proclaim the good news of Jesus Christ—declaring that He came to this world, died for our sins and was raised from the dead according to the Holy Scriptures. It is declaring Jesus as the reigning Lord who meets every human need with His forgiveness of our sins and the gift of His indwelling Holy Spirit to everyone who repents and believes. However, evangelism must conclude with a call (invitation) for repentance.

Many Christians believe that evangelism is the sole responsibility of the preacher and that the primary way to evangelize is to preach the Word from the pulpit to those who come to hear. However, few hearers are coming. Compare the increase of Christianity at an estimated annual rate of less than 10%, with Islam which is growing at a rate of 16% annually and Hinduism at 12%!

Perhaps the issue is as simple as Christian laity (non-clergy) having a fear of presenting Christ because of inexperience and rejection. They pass the responsibility for the ministry to the pastor or evangelist because of this fear. Christians tend to feel that presenting the message or good news of salvation through Jesus Christ is an imposition on others and that the unsaved neither want to hear about nor have any interest in spiritual matters.

This simply is NOT TRUE. The Bible states in Ecclesiastes 3:11 that: "He hath made everything beautiful in His time: He hath set the world in their heart,..."

This is a very interesting Scripture which many theologians believe was translated inaccurately. These theologians agree that the actual translation from the original Hebrew should read: "He has made everything beautiful in its time. He has also set eternity in the hearts of men;..."

This particular interpretation is found in both the New International Version and the new King James Version. In fact, nearly every version of the Bible interprets this Scripture the same. This leads theologians to conclude that the Lord set "eternity" into the heart of man, not the "world." This idea is strongly supported throughout the Holy Scriptures. It is the eternal things which are of the greatest value, not the things of the world.

Please do not miss the main point of this Scripture because it is the evangelist's greatest hope. Since God has placed eternity into the heart of every individual, the awareness deep down inside of us is a longing of eternity and a desire to know our Creator. This fact is true, regardless of a person's exterior appearance or attitude. In other words, it does not matter what a person says or does. He or she is hungry to know God because of intuitive interest in the reality of life after death.

When God breathed the breath of life into us, He breathed into us an inextinguishable hope of life after death. This deep-seated, universal hope is the foundation of evangelism. Coming to understand that God has placed into every man's heart an awareness of eternity certainly increases the possibility of the success of evangelism.

As stated in a popular devotional, "We do not have to convict or convince anyone; all we have to do is to wisely and lovingly strike a responsive cord in the heart of each person with whom we share the Good News. When the right cord is strummed, they will respond."

To testify is to boldly declare that God gives meaning to your life. For example, when talking with someone you can be very bold and zealous and say something like: "I do not mind telling you that everything I have, I owe to God." Or, "God has been good to me."

Evangelizing goes much further than giving one's personal testimony because it includes an invitation such as: "Would you like to pray with me right now to receive Jesus Christ as your Lord and Savior?"

THIS IS EVANGELISM and very few Christians ever do it. We may testify a hundred times a day, lay our heads on our pillow at night and feel that we have really done something for God's Kingdom. In reality, we have done little or nothing because we do not offer an invitation.

We call this planting seeds, and we usually plant enough seeds to suffocate those around us but seldom cultivate the harvest. Many Christians are simply afraid to give the invitation to, "PRAY WITH ME RIGHT NOW."

Salespersons can tell customers all day long how "Great this vacuum cleaner is." However, they will not sell it until they "close" with a statement such as: "Will you be paying in cash or do you want me to work out monthly installments?" Christians seldom "close."

One of the greatest joys for a minister or lay person is to witness to others. However, no joy can be greater than to participate in a sinner's prayer of repentance–to actually be there with the person when they pray to receive Jesus as their Lord and Savior. Concluding the witness by offering an invitation to pray "right now" will prove to be one of the most exciting and fulfilling experiences of your life.

CAUTION! You cannot pray the prayer for them, they have to say the words with their own mouth!

> *That if thou shalt confess with thy mouth the Lord Jesus, and shalt believe in thine heart that God hath raised him from the dead, thou shalt be saved. Romans 10: 9*

This was a hard lesson for me to learn. I was praying the prayer for them and letting them listen in! We would kneel down together and "I" would pray: Father, John acknowledges that he has sinned and fallen short of Your Glory and he repents.

He asks you to forgive him and to wash him in the blood of Jesus. Please come into his heart and save him Lord. Amen

Then, I saw no fruit! No change whatsoever! Why? Because I was in the way of their salvation and I was overstepping my bounds. Our part is to "listen." Their part is to make things right with their creator. What a day that will be!

This is sometimes called: "Walking down the Roman Road!"

THE BIBLE

Scripture Reference: Gen. 1: 1 – Rev. 22: 21

This book contains the mind of God, the state of man, the way of salvation, the doom of the sinner and the happiness of believers.

Its doctrines are holy, it precepts are binding, its histories are true, and its decisions are innumerable.

Read it to be wise, believe it to be safe and practice it to be holy. It contains light to direct you, food to support you and comfort to cheer you.

It is the traveler's map, the pilgrim's staff, the pilot's compass, the soldier's sword and the Christian's character. Here paradise is vested, Heaven opened and the gates of hell disclosed.

Glory of God is its end. Christ is its subject, our good its design. It should fill the memory, veil the heart and guide the feet.

Read it slowly, frequently and prayerfully. It is given to you in life, will be opened at the judgment and be remembered forever.

It involves the highest responsibility, will reward the greatest labor and condemn all who trifle with its contents.

Author Unknown

MY FRIEND

Scripture Reference: Prov. 18: 4 & 2 Cor. 13

My friend, I stand in judgment now,
    And feel that you're to blame somehow.
On earth I walked with you by day,
    And never did you point the way.
You knew the Lord in truth and glory,
    But never did you tell the story.
My knowledge then was very dim,
    You could have led me safely to Him.
Though we lived together on earth,
    You never mentioned the Second Birth.
And now I stand this day condemned,
    Because you failed to mention Him.
You taught me many things, that's true,
    I called you Friend and trusted you.
But now I learn that it's too late,
    You could have kept me from this fate.
We walked by day and talked by night,
    And yet you showed me not the Light.
You let me live and love and die,
    You knew I'd never live on high.
Yes, I called you My Friend in life,
    I trusted you thru joy and strife.
And yet on coming to this dreadful end,
    I cannot now call you, My Friend.

Author Unknown

A Blessing To The Reader

The Lord bless thee, and keep thee: The Lord make his face to shine upon thee, and be gracious unto thee: The Lord lift up his countenance upon thee, and give thee peace." Numbers 6: 24-26

Until we meet each other in Christ's glory, I bid you peace.

A Servant For Christ,
Richard G. Arno, Ph.D.

TOPICAL INDEX

TITLE INDEX

Part Two

Part Three

Part Four

SCRIPTURE INDEX

CPSIA information can be obtained at www.ICGtesting.com
Printed in the USA
LVOW100504150613

338596LV00001B/40/P